Fang Lili Chinese Ceramics

Translated by William W. Wang

CHINA
INTERCONTINENTAL
PRESS

图书在版编目（CIP）数据

中国陶瓷／方李莉著，William W. Wang译. —北京：五洲传播
出版社，2005.10（2008.1重印）
ISBN 978-7-5085-0834-4

I. 中...
II. ①方... ②W...
III. 陶瓷（工艺美术）—简介—中国—英文
IV. K876.34

中国陶瓷

撰　　文	方李莉
译　　者	Willam W. Wang
图片提供	文物出版社　《收藏家》杂志社　方李莉
特约编辑	刘美娟
责任编辑	张　宏
整体设计	海　洋
出版发行	五洲传播出版社（北京海淀区北小马厂6号　邮编:100038）
设计制作	北京锦绣东方图文设计有限公司
承 印 者	北京华联印刷有限公司
版　　次	2005年10月第1版
印　　次	2008年1月第2次印刷
开　　本	720 x 965 毫米　1/16
印　　张	9
字　　数	100千字
印　　数	8501-11500册
定　　价	92.00元

Table of Contents

1   Opening

5   Chapter 1   Primitive Colored Pottery

15   Chapter 2   Black Earthenware

21   Chapter 3   White Pottery and Primitive Porcelain

27   Chapter 4   The Terracotta Warriors and Clay Sculptures of the Qin and Han

37   Chapter 5   Millennia Celadon

49   Chapter 6   The One-of-a-Kind Tri-Colored Pottery

55   Chapter 7   The Age of Porcelain and the Five Great Kilns

69   Chapter 8   Qinghua Porcelain with Chinese Ink and Wash

85   Chapter 9   Zisha – the Taste of Tea

91   Chapter 10   Wucai Porcelain

101   Chapter 11   Fencai Porcelain

113   Chapter 12   Export Ware of the Ming and Qing Dynasties

123   Chapter 13   The Trade of the Artisans

129   Chapter 14   Contemporary Chinese Ceramics

134   Epilogue

Opening

The introduction of pottery ware signified man's subjugation of water, fire and earth. It was only possible when a certain level of technology has been attained and there was the power to transform the natural material environment. The process from emergence to application of pottery marked important milestones in the course of the refinement of living for humankind; incessantly expanding man's capacity to create applications using technology and wisdom. Ultimately, artistic objects with both functionality and aesthetic value were created.

In this age-long land, pottery brought to the people not only advancement in material culture, it also infused them rich spiritual life. Although those who created the art of pottery around ten thousand years ago have long since faded into the past, their creations left us with information of the ancient societies. If you are fascinated by history, these pieces of age-old pottery serve as the most credible evidences to history, bearing witness to an age long ago.

Around three thousand years ago was the time of the Xia and Shang Dynasties (11th-21st centuries B.C.) in China. The early Chinese discovered *Gaoling* clay, or Kaolin, from which exquisite white pottery were made. Soon after, the discovery of plant ash glaze, and by achieving higher firing temperatures, people were able to create the primitive form of porcelain based on white pottery.

By the end of the Eastern Han Dynasty (25-250 A.D.), in today's Zhejiang Province, people mixed high quality glutinous clay and pottery stone, and created a body that could be modeled and fired to create a vessel. It pale blue-green vessel was sturdy and it could be engraved or painted on for extra decoration. That was the birth of the world's earliest porcelain. Prior to the transpiration of the event, almost all early civilizations had mastered the making of pottery, but none had ever made porcelain. The rest of the areas of East Asia all learned of porcelain-making crafts from the Chinese. The Europeans did not learn of the craft until the 18th century. Thus we can proudly proclaim that China is the birthplace of porcelain and it is such a fine gift for the rest of the world indeed. The production of porcelain signified not only technological prowess, it also represented an aesthetic concept and a milestone in the orientation of cultural values. The pale green porcelain glaze, as clear as jade, is the manifestation of the Chinese tradition of "jade worship." It also represents the pursuit of "natural beauty" for the Chinese. As such, the craft of celadon porcelain continued for more than two millennia in China and was once the dominant product of Chinese porcelain art.

By the Song Dynasty (960-1279 A.D.), Chinese classical aestheticism was at its peak. There was a kind of mature rationality and self-awareness in the development and inheritance of culture. It was exactly during this time, when Han classical culture was at its prime, the art of porcelain entered an era of unprecedented prosperity. There were porcelain kilns set up all over China. Each porcelain kiln, or school of the craft, made its unique product, including the Ru kiln's celadon in sky-blue glaze and ice crackle patterns; the Imperial kiln celadon with "purple mouth and iron base;" celadon fitted with gold and iron linings by the Ge kiln; celadon of Longquan kiln that is smooth and glistening; the ever-changing and with a sunset glow porcelain from the Jun kiln; the jade-like clear celadon from Jingdezhen; the natural porcelains from Jian kiln; the shiny as silver white porcelain from Ding kiln and much more. The technology in porcelain-making enhanced tremendously, and it no longer adhered to functionality alone. The form, quality, colors, graphic designs in porcelain were all aimed for elegance, so that it had even more aesthetic appeal. Porcelain at this time fully embodied the concept of "living as an art" which was the philosophy of the elite.

As time passed, during the Yuan Dynasty (1206-1368 A.D.) when China was under the rule of the Mongols, Qinghua porcelain appeared. Under the same cultural influence as Yuan Dynasty music had, themes of popular arts, city folk arts and the multi-faceted ethnic arts soon saturated porcelain-making crafts. Although it was still not the mainstream, the newer colored porcelain which emphasized synthetic decorations was on totally opposite extremes with plain porcelain, in which people once looked for natural beauty and subtleness. The newer style gained ground in the Ming (1368-1644 A.D.) and Qing (1644-1911 A.D.) Dynasties to follow, and became fully refined. With an ever expanding foreign relations effort by the Chinese regimes, the brilliant and richly adorned colored porcelain gained not only the favors of the imperial courts, but were also exported to Europe and America far across the seas.

During the thousand years after the advent of porcelain by the hands of Chinese craftsmen, European pottery makers were never able to fully understand the art of porcelain. But the Southeastern Asian countries were taught the craft quite early on; by the 18th century, the craft was finally introduced to the Europeans. The Yuan Dynasty Qinghua porcelains were made especially for export to Islamic nations. Since the great geographical discoveries made by the European navigators in the 15th and 16th centuries, merchant fleets from European countries began to arrive at the shores of this distant, mysterious and developed civilization of the Far East, a place where they have long been interested in. The navigators from Europe saw infinite business opportunities here, with China's elegant silk and embroidery, fine tea and consummate porcelain ware mesmerizing the Europeans. Many European countries established their trade companies in India and the Far East. The Dutch East India Company played a special leading role in porcelain trade. At the end of the 16th century, porcelain ware exported to Europe through Portuguese merchants aroused so much interest, that the demand far exceeded supply and production capabilities. Through all of the 17th century, the increase in commercial exchange between Europe and China helped to promote porcelain ware as an object of exotic flare within the European upper social class. A new trend that echoed the passion for Chinese tea started to spread throughout the continent. All the way until before the 19th century, China was still the most advanced maker of porcelain. People today are able to witness the many exported fine Chinese porcelain in the museums of many countries across the world. At the same time, it is not difficult to see the impact of Chinese porcelain-making. Chinese porcelain export brought forth communication and understanding between Eastern and Western cultures and arts, and is a crucial link in the cultural development and the history of economics and commerce of humankind.

The village of Gaoling is situated near the town of Jingdezhen. On the hills behind the village is the source of clay used for porcelain making since the late-Ming Dynasty, which propelled the little village to international fame. All the way until the mid-Qing Dynasty, Jingdezhen's porcelain all relied on this porcelain clay from Gaoling Hill. It was exactly around this time that Europeans made the most frequent visits and purchase orders to Jingdezhen for importing porcelain to Europe. Since then, the entire world's porcelain-making industry universally refer to all porcelain clays as Kaolin (Gaoling), a tradition that has been carried on for over 200 years.

Ceramic products are not only an important cultural heritage of human civilization; they are still very much a part of everyone's lives, and in a very lively and colorful way. A beautifully crafted and tastefully formed ceramic piece not only is a fruit of the technology and craft of its times, it also records the bits of history and life. Sometimes, it can even carry paintings, poetry, calligraphy, sculpture all on its tiny body; or serve as a medium of information for society. A piece of ceramic ware can transcend its identity, and be a collection of the old and the new, Chinese and foreign, wholly and partial, science and aesthetics all in one; its value far exceeds its exquisite form and beautiful glaze. It is the concept of "tangible objects reveal more than the material."

Chapter **1**

Primitive Colored Pottery

Neolithic animal-shaped red earthenware pot.

Of the early civilizations in the world, almost all had gone through an age of pottery-making. The Chinese culture as one of the earliest civilizations is no exception. In the art of pottery-making in China, the most spectacular works created would be the colored pottery, which had its introduction dating from 6,000 to 7,000 years ago. The best known examples of colored pottery are those of the *Yangshao* culture (around 5000 3000 B.C., covering the northwestern part of China, with center at the middle reaches of the Yellow River); the surviving specimens today are of a red-orange color or reddish brown with maroon or black patterns. Thus the *Yangshao* culture is also known as the "colored pottery culture."

Colored pottery was an outstanding achievement of the *Yangshao* culture. The making process involves drawing or painting the patterns on the clay before the pottery vessel is fired. After firing, the colored designs are fused with the surface of the pottery and are quite resistant to fading and peeling. Colored pottery uses mostly black coloring, sometimes together with red coloring. Some areas are applied with a layer of white as the background so that painted patterns will become even more appealing. Colored pottery motifs contain subject matters including flora, geometric shapes and animals. These patterns or images are often applied to the mouths and bellies of fine-clayed alms bowls, bowls, pots and jars. Usually there would be no painted images on the underside or contracting portions of the pottery ware. This kind of design was related to the living habits of people at the time. Since people in the Neolithic Age were subject to restrictions by their living conditions, they often sat on mats directly placed on the ground or squatted. Therefore, the designs on the potteries needed to be placed at the spots most visible from such a position and angle.

Through spectral analysis of *Yangshao* culture pigments, the most prominent element in the red pigment was iron; the key elements in black coloring were iron and manganese. In white pigment, aside from small quantities of iron, there are hardly any traces of coloring. Based on these analyses, some scholars suspect that the red color was from ocher; the black pigment was made from a kind of earth with high iron content; and the white coloring was probably a derivative of porcelain clay with solvent additives.

Yangshao culture's pottery forms concentrate on both functionality and aesthetics. Its exteriors are usually fluid and balanced; with richly colored decorations, it appears unusually beautiful and has a highly artistic presence. There are many different kinds of colored pottery objects, including cups, alms bowls, bowls, pots, jars, urns, flasks, vases, cauldrons, stoves, cooking pods, and the lids and bases of vessels. Among which the small-mouthed and pointy-based vase is the most outstanding. These potteries usually show a difference in form or decorated patterns with respect to their times and places of origin.

There are many ways of shaping pottery, with the main methods being the following:

1. Pinching

This is the original and most simplistic way for making pottery. Pinched pots usually result in relatively rough and inconsistent form, but it is very flexible and convenient. Therefore is often used for small clay sculptures and only rarely employed for pottery vessels for daily use.

2. Stack-and-Shape

As with hand-pinched pottery, stack and shape is also one of the earliest ways of making pottery. By applying layers of wet and sticky clay on the outside of something akin to an inner mold, a whole vessel is shaped. Usually the pieces of clay are applied in order from bottom to top, with at least a double-layer composition; some vessels are multi-layered. Potteries made through this technique appeared thick and hefty; the shapes and especially the mouths of the vessels were not very even. From archeological findings and studies, evidence supports that stack and shape was used more than six to seven thousand years ago and was gradually replaced by the coiling technique.

3. Coiling

Pottery clay is first made into coils and then placed on top of one another in a circular fashion. Paddles other tools were used to flatten and smooth the exterior and interior, and to

Neolithic red earthenware he, *a cooking vessel.*

Colored earthenware bo, *H 20 cm. Unearthed from Dahe Village, Zhengzhou.*

accurately shape the vessel. Not only were most Neolithic pottery made this way, some minority nationality groups in China today still employ this method for pottery-making.

The making of the pottery body, in the beginning, was perhaps done on top of wooden boards, bamboo mats or bamboo baskets, to that it could be easily turned or rotated. Some were fitted with tree leaves at the bottom, thus the imprints of veins of leaves on the base of pottery vessels. Later on, a wheel that could spin was developed (slow potter's wheel), used as a rotating platform to facilitate coiling and adding decorative patterns all around the pottery. The spinning action also made the shaping and smoothing of the mouths much easier. The slow potter's wheel had drawbacks as well, as partial wheel marks are often left on the body of the pottery. This technique began roughly during the middle of the Yangshao cultural period.

Colored pottery has rich decorative images and patterns; most commonly seen are the motif of fish, birds, frogs, deer and so on, as well as some images of flora and human and deity figures. Some scholars believe that these decorative patterns were related to totem worship. In the myths and legends of ancient China, we find evidence of fish and birds being clan totems in parts of China. Among the colored potteries uncovered from the area of Banpo (6,800-6,300 years ago), a kind of large-mouthed, flare-lipped, shallow-bellied and circular-based earthen pot was found. These earthen pots usually sport black drawings with red clay coating all over the body. The interior walls of these vessels show two motifs, one with a human face and fish, the other being just a fish, all painted in black and in alternating arrangement. The human face was round; above its eyes was a black or negative triangular area. The ears either bent upwards in a symmetrical fashion or were in the shape of fishes. The fish motif was in the shape of a tall triangle, and the head of the fish was in a triangular shape as well. A round spot marked the eye of the fish and rows of diamond shapes denoted the scales. The human face and fish images alternated and interacted as two intersecting lines formed the corners of the human mouth where a fish was shown on either side. Short lines and dots decorated the body of the fish.

Colored earthenware vase unearthed from Gansu Province, H 38.4 cm, Dia. at mouth 7 cm.

Birds were the subject matter of pottery found in areas along the lower reaches of the Yellow River. From literary records found in this region, the totemic symbolism that birds carry in clan legends and records can be confirmed. Colored potteries of the later periods of the *Yangshao* culture show a dual-headed bird with multiple feet. Its body was elongated and usually appearing alongside motifs of the sun. This indicates that the clan with such a bird as its totem might have also worshipped the sun. Even though we may never know the true purpose of putting totem design and decorative patterns on pottery, we can still postulate the cause. As society progressed forward, more frequent communication occurred between all clans and tribes. The members of groups mingled with one another and thus it was difficult to differentiate their identities. Totem signs and names therefore existed to precisely distinguish groups from one another and show the different characteristics of each group. This can prevent members of one group floating to another, thus weaken the collective strength of the former, as all groups wished to become stronger. Pottery as a daily necessity of the people at the time needed to be marked with the symbol of its people, so that potteries of each group was clearly kept apart from those of other groups, and that was perhaps the true meaning of the totem sign.

In early pottery arts, we see two most common pattern types – realistic and geometric from abstraction. Most often, the earliest patterns were realistic, while geometric patterns were developed later. Take the image of the fish from potteries as an example, its earlier appearances came in forms of individual images. It was illustrated with specific traits and thus rather realistic with lesser exaggerations. These images appeared on the top section of potteries mostly. By the middle stage of colored pottery with fish patterns, the motif became more impressionistic as the head of the fish changed from natural organic forms to geometric shapes. This also increased its decorativeness. By latter stages, the fish motif was abstracted even further, eventually resulting in positive and negative geometric shapes which were highly decorative.

The image of birds on pottery pieces also experienced gradual abstraction. In the decorations found on colored pottery of the

Colored earthenware urn of the Yangshao *culture. Unearthed from Yan Village, Linru County, Henan Province.*

Miaodigou area, there are individual images of frontal or profile images of birds. The frontal view consists of a round shape signifying the head. A single triangle represents the body of the bird with wings spread. Three vertical lines denote that this is a bird with three feet. In later works, the three feet had also been omitted. Thus the bird became a logo with only two geometric shapes. The bird from a profile view began as a rather realistic image, much like a silhouette of a bird standing. As with the fontal view, the image changed from shapes to lines, then from line to simplified lines that no longer resembled a bird, but only the motion of flying remained.

Late Neolithic geometrical-lined colored earthenware basin, H 20 cm, Dia. at mouth 37.3 cm.

Colored earthenware basin of the Yangshao culture. Unearthed from the Banpo heritage site in Xi'an, Shaanxi Province.

Often appearing on colored pottery was an image that resembles a frog or a human with hands up in the air and legs in a squatting posture. Scholars seem to take sides as to whether this is the image of a frog or man. Some even believe that it could be the icon for a totemic priest dressed as a frog praying to the heavens. Other researchers believe that it was an image of people planting seeds in the fields, as a symbol of ancestral worship. This kind of semi-frog and semi-human image was later simplified, with its head omitted, and only the limbs and the fingers or paws remained. Even later, the fingers or paws were gone too and all that was left eventually were beveled lines of varying thickness.

There were many other similar cases of abstracted images in potteries of Neolithic China (6000-2000 B.C.). This would indicate

Colored earthenware pot, H 22 cm. Unearthed from Dahe Village in Zhengzhou.

that the patterns on colored pottery of this particular era abode strongly by an ordinance. They were not simply icons denoting certain tribes or clan, nor were they merely religious patterns. It also had the functions of written languages.

Through deciphering these primitive colored pottery motifs, we can perhaps return to the origins of Chinese philosophy. Primitive potteries from other countries of the world also had patterns that were either realistic or geometric. The geometric patterns were usually symmetrical or arranged in tiers; some had a uniform spatial arrangement. Most of those images were of a static state. However, images found on Chinese colored pottery usually signified motion. There were many curved lines and round shapes, which brought forth a sense of frolic and movement. Usually this type of movement came in a spiraling fashion and repetitive cycle; a swirl motif gives off a sense of constant motion, which transcends the limitations of space. This may very well have been the reflection of the early people's macro-understanding of the universe.

In addition, pottery found at the Banpo area near present day Xi'an often contained Yin and Yang decorations, or positive and negative markings. Not only does it possess a strong decorative effect, it also conveys the concept of the opposites, which attract, interact and exist because of the other. The Banpo area was where the ancient Zhou people once dwelled, and the originating area of the concept of Yin and Yang. Therefore it should be no mere coincidence that such designs found their way onto pottery. At the time, colored pottery spinning wheels, used for textiles, also

Colored earthenware pot of the Majiayao culture (some 5,000 years ago). Unearthed from Lintao, Gansu Province.

contained many "S-shaped" lines, dividing its round surface into halves. They seem to be revolving concentrically, which is really the basic concept of Yin Yang. Such a movement can represent the heaven and earth, the sun and moon, man and woman and everything else in the universe, as opposites balance and constantly interact with one another.

The design patterns on colored pottery of the late-Neolithic Age are the earliest cases of large-scale creation of geometric patterns in Chinese history. As a message carrier, they revealed to us the richness of early Chinese culture, including social order and discipline which should have begun to develop at the same time. As an art form, they laid the cornerstone for decorative patterns to be used in a wide range of media and applications. Many ways of creating decorative patterns were all fully realized during this time, such as band patterns consisting of with two combined units; or uniformly placed repeating patterns with four combined units; rules of symmetry, balance and contrast, and changes within harmony; the ways to create individual motifs and fitting designs within particular shapes; the proper use of points, lines, shapes and areas of black, white and grey and so on. This time period can be considered a peak of development in the history of Chinese decorative pattern design.

Chapter **2**

Black Earthenware

Among primitive Chinese potteries, aside from colored potteries, the black earthenware had also attained considerable refinement in technique and artistically. Black pottery first appeared around 2000 B.C., and was based on the colored pottery. It was during the transitional period from primitive society to slave society in China that black pottery was created. Be it religious or ancestral rituals, everything at that time was developing towards a more standardized and systematic direction. The members of society had a clearer

Black earthenware basin of the Hemudu *culture (some 7,000 years ago), H 11.7 cm, Dia. 17.5 - 21.7 cm at mouth. The collection of Zhejiang Museum.*

differentiation of social status, and political and economic interests also needed to be systematically distributed among them.

The clay used for black pottery, as the material for colored pottery, was of the finest kind. Though black potteries were still handmade, most were produced on a fast potter's wheel (kick wheel), an improvement from its slow counterpart from the colored pottery period. The use of jiggers was also quite common. At this time, aside from a small quantity of potteries and the different attached parts such as the ears, nose, mouths, handles and support, which were still formed by hand, the

16

main bodies of most potteries were crafted with the help of the potter's wheel. It not only has the advantage of producing more uniform and consistent shapes, the thickness of the pottery can also be controlled more precisely. Thus, the black pottery, with their eggshell-thin bodies, can be made without difficulty. The surface of black pottery received a polished finish, which was accomplished by pressing and polishing the surface of the near-dried body with conglomerates or tools of bone. When the body was fired, its exterior became quite shiny. Colored pottery also received such a treatment before patterns were painted. The black pottery was the successor to this technique and its shiny texture and thin body captures our imaginations.

The emergence of black pottery was intimately related to changes in firing technology and kiln atmosphere. Pottery made from iron-rich clay would produce red or brown colors when fired in an oxidation atmosphere, and would turn black when fired with in a reduction atmosphere. The primitive firing technique required heating the kiln up to a required temperature and blocking the smoke passage. Thus the kiln would be deficient of oxygen enough for the iron element in the clay to be reduced, causing the pottery to turn black. Since such technique required a higher kiln temperature and a level of control over the degree of fire, we determine that kiln technology has advanced a considerable step by this time. By measurement, kilns producing black pottery can reach maturing temperatures of 1,000 degrees Celsius, while colored potteries were fired at temperatures of roughly 800 degrees.

Black pottery, while benefiting from finer clay, fast potter's wheel, polished finish, advanced firing techniques and more, stood apart from all other potteries before it. Better firing brought forth better compactness and coagulation of the clay material, which in turn increased the rigidity of the body. The fast potter's wheel not only produced thinner and more uniform bodies, but made numerous forms and shapes not seen in colored pottery possible.

With changes in firing and forming techniques taking place, changes were bound to follow in form design and decorative

Black earthenware pot of the Liangzhu culture, H 15 cm. The collection of the Shanghai Museum.

*Neolithic black earthenware vase, H 25 cm. Unearthed from Qingpu
County in Shanghai. Collection of the Shanghai Museum.*

styling of pottery. First, from a decorative art standpoint, the surfaces of black pottery were not suitable for colored decorations; its more complex shapes were also difficult to paint on. In most black potteries, which were intended for practical use, often seen was the polished finish, as it was a very elegant and refined way of enhancing its beauty. By taking advantage of the fast potter's wheel and jigger, all kinds of raised or incised parallel line patterns can be applied to the surface. These marks not only served to divide the pottery object into different sections, they were also a kind of adornment and the unique styling feature of black pottery. The excitement, passion and wildly imaginative decorative motifs of the colored pottery gave way for the orderly, sequential and highly precise parallel line patterns. The warm color combination of red, black and yellow found on colored pottery was also replaced by the monotonous but sophisticated black. Those repeating parallel lines found on black pottery, especially of goblets, which were full of rhythm, melody and movement, contained a form of beauty based on programmed patterns. If colored pottery represents passionate and impulsive beauty, then black pottery equals to rational aesthetics.

By way of modeling and artistic styling, the potter's wheel and jigger gave pottery wares many more variations to the exterior contours. Since colored pottery emphasized the paintings and patterns on its surface, its exterior contour was usually very simple and full. However, black pottery, with no painted décor on the outside, fully relied on its undulating surfaces. Therefore, the utmost attention was put into the design and making of the exterior form of black pottery. It was apparent in the transitions from mouth to shoulder, shoulder to belly and belly to feet of the pottery; every bit of detail showed the pursuit for variations. If we say that colored pottery is an art relying on decorations, then black pottery stands firm with shape and form that is ever changing.

During the colored pottery period, containers made for daily living were limited to jars, kettles, teapots, alms bowl, bowls, vases, cups and so forth. The advent of the fast potter's wheel gave life to new types of pottery vessels during the black pottery period, including the *Yan* for cooking foods and the high-footed *Dou*, a container designed to facilitate people's reach and access while sitting on the floor. In terms of decorations, besides the usual polished treatment, the surfaces of black pottery can be adorned with all kinds of etched patterns, parallel line patterns, basket patterns, geometric patterns, finger nail patterns, circular patterns and carved aperture patterns and so on.

Chapter 3

White Pottery and Primitive Porcelain

White pottery gui *of the* Longshan *culture. Unearthed from Weifang, Shandong Province.*

Among early Chinese potteries, the white pottery was particularly worthy of notice. It is not only because of the uniquely clean and pure beauty that it possessed; another very important reason is that its raw material was quite different from most clay and sand potteries at that time. Abundant information shows that the white pottery's chemical properties were very close to those of porcelain clay and Kaolin. There was a minute difference in iron content between porcelain clay and Kaolin, 1.59 percent and 1.72 percent respectively, both much lower than other raw clay used for pottery-making. Thus the white pottery, similar to these two kinds of materials, also gained the white color.

White pottery surfaces usually have the polished finish, with only few examples of the stamped rope patterns. The late-Shang Dynasty was the time of rapid development in the making of white pottery. The works during this time used fine quality body that was white and smooth. On the surfaces are engraved with unique Chinese patterns such as *Taotie*, *Kui*, *Yunlei*, and more. It is also evident that some white potteries were imitations of bronze wares of the same time period, having similar or identical modeling and adorning motifs. The firing technique for white pottery was the most advanced of all pottery at the time. Compare to other potteries, white pottery was sturdier in material, cleaner and more elegant in appearance; thus it was the favorite among the ruling class. During the Xia (21st-17th centuries B.C.) and Shang dynasties, white potteries were mostly Chinese wine containers owned by the ruling class, such as the *gui*, *he* and *jue* or vessels for foods such as the *Dou* and *Bo*,

The significance of white pottery lies in its use of porcelain-class clay. Although white pottery was not yet true porcelain as kiln technology was still insufficient, but it most certainly paved the way for the creation of primitive porcelain. The ancient Chinese, when making white pottery and hard stamped pottery, sought constant improvements in body materials and tempering; added with increased maturing temperatures and better glazing techniques, the end result was primitive porcelain.

There were three basic requisites to producing primitive porcelain. First was the choice of raw material and treatment;

White pottery Ding, *Imitating bronze.*

Primitive porcelain gui, H 12 cm. Spring and Autumn Period. Unearthed from Changzhou in Jiangsu Province. Collection of the Changzhou Municipal Museum in Jiangsu Province.

increased aluminum oxide content and lowered iron oxide concentration was needed so that the body can be of a white color. The second requirement was maturing temperatures of at least 1,200 degrees Celsius, so that the body can be fully congealed and no longer water-absorbent; when knocked on, it produced a crisp metallic ring. Third and last requirement was the glaze, which was applied uniformly to the body and also fired at high temperatures.

The creation of glaze was certainly an essential condition for making porcelain ware. The glaze on primitive porcelain was perhaps discovered by chance. While firing a piece of pottery inside a tightly sealed kiln with rather high temperatures, some burnt wood ash came into contact with the surface of the pottery, and was melted and congealed with the feldspar in the porcelain clay. Thus a thin layer of natural glaze was formed. This accidental occurrence gave pottery-makers an innovative idea. They proceeded to mix firewood ash with diluted porcelain clay, and applied the mixture on the surface of unfired clay body. That was how early ash glaze was born. This type of glaze which contained firewood ash and small traces of iron turned yellow or brown in oxidation fire, and blue or blue-green in reduction fire. High-temperature glazing can be considered a great invention of the Chinese people, albeit accidental, its discovery was even earlier than the first practice of low temperature glazing, which was invented in West Asia. Usually in basic colors of olive green, green, blue-green, blue, yellow and brown, high temperature glaze, when compared to the exquisite low-temperature glazes in West Asia and southern Europe, appeared more calm, subtle, elegant and soothing. This characteristic later became a unique style of Chinese porcelain.

Primitive porcelain wares usually came in vessels such as wine cups, *lei*, bowl, urn, jar, *dou*, *gui* and so on. Its body was relatively tough and usually in a grayish white or grayish brown color. Very few pieces have bodies of off-white with a slight yellowish tint. Its glaze color was usually blue-green; some were bean green, dark green or yellow green. The modeling of primitive porcelain was the same as hard stamped pottery, which

Shang Dynasty zun *(wine vessel) with parallel line patterns and green glaze, H 18 cm, Dia. 19.65 cm at mouth. Collection of the Shanghai museum.*

was made through the coil method. After achieving desired shape, stamps engraved with design patterns would be used to slap the surface of the body. On one hand, it strengthens the bond of the clay coils. On the other hand, decorative patterns were impressed onto the cast. Finally, the vessel was smoothed, glazed and fired. Primitive porcelain were rarely plain under the glazed surface, most were covered with geometric patterns such as leaf veins, sawteeth marks, parallel lines, mat crossings and s-shapes, some would be circular or rope patterns.

The newly introduced primitive porcelain in the Shang Dynasty had many great qualities. Its surface had a smooth glaze, which was somewhat resistant to dirt and easy to clean. Aside from the middle to lower reaches of the Yellow River where small quantities of primitive porcelain was unearthed, most archeological findings of primitive porcelain were concentrated around the lower reaches of the Yangtze River and southeastern China along the coast.

Chapter 4

The Terracotta Warriors and Clay Sculptures of the Qin and Han

The word *Yong* in Chinese was derived from the ancient funerary custom of "deal with death just as with life." To provide the deceased with an environment just as in real life so that the dead can "live" their afterlife, figurines representing servants, guards and performers were all created as burial objects. These tomb figurines as well as toys in the shape of animals were collectively referred to as *Yong*.

The Qin (221-206 B.C.) and Han (206 B.C.-220 A.D.) Dynasties were the early phases in the development of Chinese feudal society; it was the crucial period when all the nationalities of China, through a process of mergence, established a country of multiple nationalities. We saw in Qin Dynasty for the first time in history the unification of China. Qin Shihuangdi as the first emperor signified that the Qin Dynasty under his reign was

Qin Dynasty terracotta statue with colored paintings.

unprecedented in scale and power. His armies also commanded great honor and imposing manner due to the national spirit of his era. Such a spirit can be seen in the art forms of the time.

The great discovery made in 1974 truly shocked the world. With its unprecedented artistic expression and grandness of scale, the terracotta warriors uncovered near the tomb of Qin Shihuangdi are a treasure to human civilization. Several thousand lifelike and life-sized human and horse sculptures dressed in war armor were presented in formation. There were forward combat warriors, foot soldiers, cavalries and chariots, as well as guard troops at the flanks. In groups of four, robust terracotta steeds were seen with well-equipped war chariots, armor-clad soldiers and caped warriors with sophisticated weapons. This was obviously an intricate troop formation of the Qin military, with the combination of infantry and vehicle units. The terracotta warriors gave us a visual representation of the Qin military might and its all-powerful ruler.

These terracotta sculptures were made with combined techniques of molding and

Terracotta horse chariot unearthed from the tombs of Qin Shihuangdi.

modeling, and were created first in parts and then assembled. The different parts were connected to form a rough body and fine clay is applied to the surface. With modeling, pinching, piling, plastering, carving and painting, each of the several thousand soldiers of different ages and ranks were made to resemble unique personalities. One can almost tell their hometowns from their very detailed and specific appearances. All the warriors wore plated armors with belts fastened and hair tied in a knot, ready to conquer the battlefields. Some soldiers held bows and crossbows in their hands with pouches full of arrows carried on their backs. Others held long spears with swords and scimitar. Still others were middle-aged strongmen with jagged beards and mustache or younglings with unrelenting energy. Look closely and one can even find, among the warriors, long-bearded elders with thinned faces; or fearless fighters who can overcome anything in their way. The commanders' forms were the most successful and astounding, with tall helmets, intricate armor and long broadswords, immersed in deep contemplation. Let's not forget the 1.5-meter tall, 2-meter long terracotta horses. The horses were typical of the Qin Dynasty,

Clay ceremonial guard figure, H 49 cm. Western Han Dynasty. Collection of the Xuzhou Museum, Jiangsu Province.

Western Han Dynasty clay horse carriage.

Eastern Han Dynasty clay spectator figure

stout with small ears and large eyes; their bodies were in a very flexible stance, yet with staunch physique. The horses and soldiers together brought out even more power and prestige to the battle array. The Qin terracotta warriors were truly the masterpiece in the history of ancient Chinese sculptures. The Qin artisan, with their superb artistic creativity and awesome display for realistic modeling, left later generations with an immensely astonishing work of art.

The Han Dynasty was the period of great development for Chinese sculptural. The categories, numbers, body and technical quality of figures produced at this time have all reached unprecedented high levels. However, after entering the Western Han Dynasty, those life-sized sculptures found in Qin Shihuangdi's tomb have already become a thing of the past. The Han Dynasty emperors' tombs were based on the tomb of Qin Shihuangdi, however the Han tomb figurines, albeit matching in quantity with the Qin, were reduced considerably in size. The average height was usually 50 to 60 cm. In the first year of the Western Han Dynasty (206 B.C.-25 A.D.), there were already two general kinds of clay figure in existence. One kind completely replicated those of the Qin tomb figures, where the clothing and

Eastern Han Dynasty clay acrobat figure

31

Clay woman figure. Six dynasties.

accessories were directly formed out of clay. The second type was drastically different as the figures represented naked bodies of men and women, which were dressed in real costumes and clothing later on.

In the Han Dynasty, aside from tombs of emperors, which had the privilege to be buried with clay armies in formation, highly renowned generals also enjoyed the company of statues in military formation when entombed. Other high officials and the emperor's next of kin had tombs smaller in size compared to the emperor, but had in addition to protective warrior statues, also clay figures of family servants and performers. By the Eastern Han Dynasty (25-220 A.D.), with the development of a plantation farming economy, powerful and influential landlords begin to play a greater role in the political arena. In their burials grounds were scaled-down, group clay sculptures that imitated real scenes of farm production and daily living, which were even more vivid and convincing.

By mid-Western Han Dynasty, pottery figures began to show a new style, with bolder and freer sculpting techniques, no longer confined by the style of detailed human feature depiction that was prevalent in Qin and early Han sculptures. The newer style was more focused on overall simplicity and suggestive forms. Also, the subject matter and object forms were also more inclusive and varied; more depictions of folk living and amusement can be found. In 1969 a Han tomb found in the northern suburbs of Jinan City contained colored pottery sculptures of arts performers and audiences, all in one group. These clay figures were all made out of molds, with a layer of white powder as prime, and painted on top in red, black, brown, green and so on. This sculpture group was placed on top of a rectangular earthenware plate that was 67 cm in length and 47.5 cm in width. Against a backdrop of a musical band with all sorts of instruments and performers, a dance and acrobatics troupe comprising of both males and females took up center stage. On the sides were seven spectators in long robes and sleeves watching attentively. In the entire scene, the performers, spectators and the band players were arranged in a very orderly

Eastern Han Dynasty clay vocalist figure.

Foreign musician playing drum on camelback. Clay sculpture. Tang Dynasty.

fashion, placing the correct emphasis on the respective objects. This was a very vivid scene of entertainment performance for the loyalty, displayed so realistically that it makes one feel to be a part of the actual scene. The creator of this sculpture group tried to capture the people's spirits and movements, but not overly focused on the facial expressions and details of people. Therefore the figures were rough yet loveable. The subject matter of this clay sculpture group was no longer a scene of laboring of household servants, but instead replaced by an occasion of music and dance. It reflected changes in the lifestyles and choice of indulgence and amusement of the aristocratic class.

From Western Han to Eastern Han, the subject matters of pottery figures have become even more rich and inclusive. There were models of carriages hauled by handsome stallions, as well as throngs of male and female servants, music and dancer performers and so on, all of which were common subject matters for making sculptures at the time. The most vivid and memorable pieces among the so-called "100 performance artists" sculptures uncovered so far at Chengdu suburbs had to be the "vocalist figures," which were all depicted top-naked. Also famous were figurines of dancers, wind instrument performers, sitting figurines, and more. The sword-wielding figurine, drummer figurine and string instrument figurines found in Chongqing City were all very lively and realistic, full of the essence of daily

Man playing string instrument, H 36 cm. Clay sculpture. Eastern Han Dynasty. Collection of the Guizhou Museum.

living. Furthermore, animal sculptures of the Han Dynasty were also very successful. Examples such as the clay horses and canines from Mianyang, Sichuan Province; and the 1.5-meter-tall horses and carriages from Chengdu; as well as a batch of animal sculptures from Hui County, Henan Province, all fully demonstrated the different posture and attitudes of the all kinds of animals.

Not only were statues of warriors, secretarial officials and music and acrobatic performers still being produced by this time, more simulated architecture and farmland scenes were modeled into pottery. There would be many clay sculptures depicting laborers in the fields, as well as miniaturized farms and even rice paddies. The farmers were shown to be carrying spades and shouldering hoes and so on; some were equipped with long swords at the waist. These were the images of farmers, who worked for large and powerful clans in the late Eastern Han period, functioning as both farm workers and armed guards for their masters. There were also figures of domestic servants serving tea, dusting the furniture and ornaments and sweeping the floor; or kitchen helpers who are gutting fish. The clay figures showed development of a plantation farming economy in a special feudal era. At the same time, it demonstrated that the Han Dynasty, different from the Qin, pursued pragmatism in aesthetics.

Chapter 5

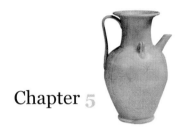

Millennia Celadon

(Left) *Porcelain chicken-headed ewer with brown glaze from Deqing kiln, H 27 cm, Dia. 8.5 cm at mouth, Dia. 12 cm at base. East Jin Dynasty.*
(Middle) *Colored-spotted ewer on black ground. Tang Dynasty.*
(Right) *Celadon pot with brown appliqued figurines of Changsha kiln. Tang Dynasty.*

Almost all peoples in this world had some sort of history making pottery, but the creation of porcelain was not a feat achievable by all. Foremost, porcelain-making required relatively high firing temperatures, which called for kilns with sophisticated designs and excellent temperature-keeping capabilities, as well as proper fuel to generate sufficient heat. Secondly, mastery in selection of porcelain-quality clay and the production and application of high-temperature glaze was required. What seemed easy in theory was actually quite difficult to achieve; the Chinese discovered and mastered these techniques first.

Here we cannot do without mentioning of a special type of kiln – the Dragon kiln. Backed by evidence from archeological findings, this type of kiln first appeared during the Warring States Period (475-221 B.C.) in the city of Zengcheng in Guangdong Province. Then there was the Eastern Han Dynasty Dragon kiln in the Shangyu area of Zhejiang Province, which is better known today. This kind of kiln was likely to have been an evolution of the rising-heat kilns which consisted of a fire chamber linked to the kiln compartment. The top of the Dragon kiln was sealed and the kiln was tilted; with the lower end being the fire chamber and a smoke vent was located at the highest position. The kiln was constructed against mountain slopes; its shape hinted at the mystical animal of the dragon, hence the name. The advantages of the Dragon kiln was its capability to rapidly increase and decrease temperature, and being able to quickly reach and maintain a reduction atmosphere. The Dragon kiln of the Eastern Han Dynasty can already reach a maturing temperature of over 1,200 degrees Celsius; the porcelain produced had glazing that was even and absent from cracks. The glaze was of a light green color and the body was white and refined. The thinner parts of the body were translucent and the glaze was tightly bonded to body. This kind of porcelain had water absorbency from 0.5 to 0.16 percent. In some abandoned

Celadon sculpture of storage house. The Three Kingdoms period. Ezhou Museum of Hubei Province.

kiln sites, fine pieces of green porcelain, or celadon, were discovered. The history of porcelain in China and even for the world has begun a brand new chapter.

The new breed of porcelain industry grew rapidly, as the making of celadon during the 3rd to 6th centuries became the fastest growing handicraft business in China; it was soon to become a new school of art that was to span across all of China. The southern style celadon were mainly produced in Zhejiang, Jiangsu, Jiangxi, Hunan, Anhui, Sichuan, Hubei and other southern provinces; the production of celadon in the north were concentrated in the provinces of Shaanxi, Hebei, Henan and Shandong. Celadon for a long period of time was the dominant product of the Chinese porcelain industry.

Why is it, that celadon gained such unanimous praise from the Chinese, and even as to usher in accolade from the Korean peninsula, Japan and southeastern Asian

Celadon pot with tray-shaped mouth. West Jin Dynasty.

countries? It seems that we should be looking for the answer on a philosophical and aesthetic level – the jade-like color and body of the celadon was perhaps more suited for Chinese taste. Jade in Chinese eyes is the epitome of beauty, infused with the essence of the sun and moon, and is a medium to the spiritual world. Therefore, since days of old, the Chinese have adored jade. Especially in remote antiquity, jade was once an important object of ceremonies. The Chinese character "*li*", meaning etiquette and ceremony, found on early bronze inscriptions appeared as the pictograph of a vessel containing two strands of jade objects. This signified that the vessels of sacrificial rites in ancient times were mostly made of jade. In addition, jade was also a charm worn by emperors and people of high status. However, for the common people, jade was a rare item and was extremely difficult to craft. Thus naturally, people sought for the jade-like beauty in celadon, which had very similar color and body as jade.

The province of Zhejiang, with large production volumes of celadon, has been viewed as the originating place of this type of porcelain. Looking back at the history of celadon, the prestigious celadon kilns in the Tang Dynasty included Yue, Wuzhou, Ou and Deqing kilns. By the Song Dynasty, there were new developments in celadon-making, with characteristic kilns being the Longquan kilns, Yaozhou kilns and the city of Jingdezhen.

The Yue kilns there were the fastest developing of all celadon kilns, with the most number of sites and coverage area, and the best quality products. The Yue kilns influenced the areas around it and became the leading force in development of celadon. The name "Yue" kiln should have come from the Tang Dynasty, which usually referred to kiln sites and products by the locations of the kilns. The name "Yue" kilns was really just short for "Yuezhou (a city name)" kilns. The Yue kilns were situated at the northeastern part of Zhejiang Province. It was the general name for all kilns that produce celadon around the Yuyao Shanglin Lake area. The most characteristic kiln was the Shanglin Lake kiln (30 km northeast of present day Yuyao County). The Yue kilns produced many categories of products, including jars, spittoons, wine pots, incense burners, cups, bowls, flasks, cases, writing-brush basins, dishes, handle-less cups, pots, wine cups, flat bowls, basins and so on, as well as children's toys such as porcelain dogs, ponies and chicks.

Production of celadon from Yue kilns relied on Dragon kiln technology. The key material was porcelain stone, which is the mixture of mica, quartz and other elements. It was equivalent to the compound of Kaolin, feldspar and quartz, which is low in organic substances and has comparatively low viscosity and absorbency. Its impurities of mica minerals also made its iron content rather high (0.5%-3%). The type of limestone glaze applied to celadon was highly lustrous and had good transparence and hardness. Only the reduction fires of the Dragon kiln can create such glass-like transparence with a glaze material that had such a low melting point and viscosity, so that all the engraved motifs, patterns or relief on the body can clearly

Cup in green glaze with etched patterns, H 13.2 cm, Yue kiln. Collection of the Suzhou Municipal Museum of Jiangsu Province.

Yue kiln flower-shaped dish, H 6.2 cm. Tang Dynasty. Unearthed from Famen Temple, Shaanxi Province. Collection of the Shaanxi Famen Temple Museum.

41

Chinese Ceramics

appear before peoples' eyes. Celadon of the Yue kilns were all fired at temperatures above 1,200 degrees Celsius; in some cases as high as 1,300 degrees. Judging from the body and glaze, early Yue celadon had a finely-textured body usually in gray or white; it was fired to a fully congealed hardness and no longer water absorbent. The body was completely covered in a highly uniform layer of glaze. The glazed areas were different depending on the vessel and its use: bowls, drinking cups, flat bowls, and basins all have full inner glaze and its outer glaze was to the base where the body was left untouched; kettles, jars and other vessels were glazed including areas around the mouth and all of the exterior, while the interior was left to bare. Since the body's color was complementary to the color of the glaze, therefore early celadon had a light-colored body and greenish glaze. However, later celadon had thicker bodies that were deeper in tone; the glaze was thicker to match and still applied very uniformly; the celadon appeared grayish-green. The common ways of decorating a Yue celadon would be etched, carved, sculpture, pierced patterns and so on. Decorative motifs included the parrot, dragon, phoenix, butterflies, birds, flowers as well as famous personages.

Yue porcelains, with advantages of a long tradition, strong technological support and superior materials, gained the honor of "King of All Kilns" among all celadon categories throughout China. A certain class of the finest Yue porcelains was custom made as tribute for the imperial court. At the time, many poets have created romancing poetry praising the porcelain from the Yue kilns; their vivid language glorified the colors and luster of the Yue porcelain. The celadon of Shanglin Lake Yue kiln was widely acclaimed, as we can find records of these products from Japanese literary annals of the Meiji Period. A Japanese poet by the last name of Ishikawa wrote in his Kanji poems about the history and glaze colors of celadon from Shanglin Lake. Through Minzhou (Ningbo) harbor, a constant supply of Shanglin Lake celadon was shipped to Korea and Japan in East Asia, as well as to Arab nations in West Asia. Until this day, there exists in India, Iran, Egypt, Japan and other countries, unearthed celadon that were made originally in Shanglin Lake.

Wuzhou kiln was situated at the central Jinhua region of

Yue kiln lobed ewer.
Tang Dynasty.

present day Zhejiang Province. Porcelain kilns spread throughout the area and had broad coverage. With archeological research, a total of more than 600 ancient kiln sites were discovered, which were built from the Han to Ming dynasties. This discovery unveiled unusually numerous kilns which have been in service for the longest times, and held a relatively significant spot in the history of ceramics. Early specimens of Wuzhou kiln porcelain had glazes in light gray and were rather rough. It had poorly tempered and under-vitrified clay with irregularities on the surface. Speckles often formed on the glaze of Wuzhou porcelain; they were green or sometimes with yellow mixed in. The many crackles on the surface, which often contained protruding yellow crystallized matters, were a unique feature of Wuzhou porcelain. By the middle phase of the development of Wuzhou kiln porcelain, porcelain clay resources in the area

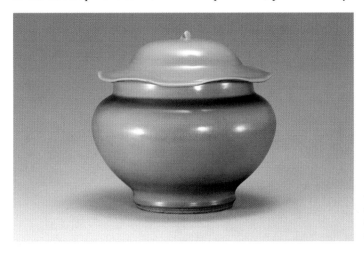

Bowl with lid in plum-green glaze with lotus petal patterns. Longquan kiln. Song Dynasty.

have become scattered and thinned out, making it difficult to mine. Therefore, the craftspeople used local red clay, which were easily mined, to model the bodies of vessels. But since red clay had high iron oxide and titanium oxide content levels, it became dark purple after being fired, undermining the quality of the greenish glaze. Therefore, a layer of fine white dressing clay was used to cover the body. With the cosmetic clay underneath, the glaze appeared smooth and soft, showing a bit of brown in green or yellow green. However, the crackling and crystallization in the glaze was even more apparent when compared to porcelain wares that had porcelain clay for the bodies. During the late period of Wuzhou kilns, new models and types of porcelain vessels were created, which better exemplified the shiny glaze quality on top of thinner bodies. There were also new breakthroughs in decorative methods.

The Ou kilns lay in the southern part of Zhejiang Province in the Wenzhou area. To its east were the great seas and its southern neighbor was Fujian Province; on the northwest were the Kuocang Mountains from which the Oujiang and Feiyunjiang Rivers flowed straight out to sea. This area was one of ancient China's business ports; porcelain, shipbuilding, embroidery and other handicrafts were all booming businesses here. Most of the Ou kilns were concentrated along the banks of Oujiang, Feiyunjiang and Nanxijiang Rivers. As early as the Han Dynasty, the Yongjia area on the north shore of the Oujiang River produced primitive porcelain, which evolved into celadon by the end of the Eastern Han Dynasty. The products were transported by boats and rafts to Wenzhou and other cities for sale; transportation by waterway was convenient and efficient. The body of Ou porcelain was whitish with a hint of grey. The glaze was slightly green and with high transparence. With such color and luster, products of the Ou kilns were also called *Piao* porcelains, for their unpredictable beauty.

While the Yue kilns were at the height of its glory and popularity, the Deqing kilns, famed for its black and shiny porcelain ware, became a capable complement to the Yue kilns. Deqing kilns produce glazed black porcelain, as well as celadon. Its ancient sites lied within Deqing County in Zhejiang Province, with as many as a dozen kilns sites. It was also one of the earliest discovered production areas of black porcelain in Zhejiang. Its products of black porcelain and celadon were simplistic and subtle, yet sophisticated and presentable. The style of Deqing porcelain products was similar to those of Wuzhou and Yue kilns. The main vessel types included bowls, dishes, plates, ear-shaped cups, broad-mouthed urns, chicken-head post, spittoons, incense burners, jars, boxes, lamps and cup holders and so on, all were objects of daily necessity. Some special products included cylindrical jars with lids, round and flat cases, as well as tea cups and complete tea ware sets. These special vessels were rare among porcelain kilns of the same time period. Deqing kilns' black porcelains had relatively thick glaze that were either dark brown or brown sienna. The better quality pieces had smooth and glistening glazed surfaces that were as black as night. Celadon was mostly covered in dressing clay on top of its body, and with a bean-green, blue green or yellow-blue glaze. The glaze was deep and quite glossy with only simple decorations;

Longquan kiln celadon Yuhuchun vase. Song Dynasty. Yuhuchun vase has flare lip, thin neck, droopy belly and round base. Its soft, curved shape was first established in the Song Dynasty, and its production continued to the present day, becoming a characteristic type of Chinese porcelain vessel.

Longquan kiln celadon ewer. Ming Dynasty.

*Pierced incense burner
with leaf scroll patterns.
Yue kiln. Northern Song
Dynasty.*

usually the rim of the mouth, the belly and shoulder would be impressed with parallel lines patterns. Judging from archeological findings, Deqing porcelain's history can be traced back for at least 6,000 years. Subsequent generations continued its porcelain crafts; however, the Deqing kilns were only active for over a century and then faded out of the spotlight. As a consequence, porcelain wares of the Deqing kilns preserved to the present day are extremely rare. Collections of Deqing porcelain can be found in the Shanghai Museum and other large-scale museums throughout China. However, having a Deqing porcelain can make any private collector smile with joy; especially the black chicken-headed jar which earns top spot on the list of every collector.

The Longquan kilns were considered one of the most characteristic kilns of the Song Dynasty, its location was also in Zhejiang Province, with kilns at Longquan Dayao, Jincun and so forth. It was established during the Five Dynasties Period and inherited the traditions of the Yue kilns, mainly in the discipline of celadon production. By the Southern Song Dynasty (1127-1279 A.D.), Longquan kilns have reached its prime. Longquan celadon excelled in the texture and color of the glaze. Thick and smooth, the glaze was as beautiful as jade, and came in many colors such as moon white, pea green, light blue, blue gray, crab-shell red, grayish yellow, cream and so on. The most attractive were Fenqing and plum green glazes. Glazed Fenqing Longquan porcelain appeared slightly turbid, light milky green in color and was easy on the eyes. Plum green glaze was deeper and lustrous in comparison; it was jade green with spots of transparency, much like a fresh sour plum. The creation of these two glaze colors depended on improvements in firing technology and porcelain crafts. Longquan porcelain used not lime glaze but alkaline-calcareous glaze instead; an obviously innovative improvement. By doing this, the glaze can be thick yet fully congealed, so that air bubbles would expand. The surface of the glaze was soft and elegant, giving the porcelain qualities of jade. Longquan porcelain wares had complex designs and forms. Aside from vessels for daily use, porcelain stationery and retrospective porcelain were also produced, which included vases, *gu*, cooking vessels, stoves and so on. As for decorative patterns, there were newly added embossed sculptures and appliqué patterns. Yuan Dynasty Longquan porcelains were shipped and exported overseas in mass quantities; more kilns were set up to meet with increased demand. By mid-Qing Dynasty however, the Longquan kilns met with decline and ceased production. It was not until 1949 did the Longquan kilns regain its former glory and began making porcelain once again.

Yaozhou kilns were established in the Tang Dynasty, its product line included black, celadon and white porcelains. From the Five Dynasties Period to early Song Dynasty, it was influenced by the Yu, Yao and Yue kilns and developed celadon with engraved designs. It was one of the best known celadon kilns in the north of China. The remaining site of Yaozhou kilns was found at Huangbao Town, Tongchuan City in Shaanxi Province. In the old days, this area belonged to the Yaozhou government. Its products can be distinguished by three development stages. The earliest phase produced mostly celadon and the modeling was rather simple; designs and patterns were still quite amateur in execution and layout. In the present day, there are more surviving Yaozhou wares from the second stage than any other, as the second stage was at the height of development Yaozhou kilns. Most of the products from this time were daily necessities such as bowls and dishes. There were also every other imaginable vessel such as vases, jars, kettles, basins, stoves, incense burners, cup holders, flat bowls, wine pot, wine pot warmer and more. The richness in variety of form and model was something that few could contend with in the Song Dynasty. Its carved patterns on Yaozhou celadon showed strength,

Underside-loading ewer with green glaze and etched patterns, H 19 cm. Yaozhou Kiln. Song Dynasty. Collection of the Shaanxi Museum of History.

precision and fluidity in knife work and represented a unique style. The motif of fish in the sea and frolicking duck by lotus pond were some of the most vivid images. In addition to carved designs, imprinted designs were also quite common for Yao porcelain. Commonly used patterns and designs included floral scrolls or floral sprays of peonies, chrysanthemum, lotuses and so on. Sometimes, images such as lotuses, phoenixes and peonies, flying cranes, flying moths and all kinds of frolicking children motifs were used. Yaozhou products were geared towards the common people. With its unique local style, top rate quality and style among porcelain products of its category in northern China, Yaozhou celadon had was selected as yearly tribute ware for the Northern Song (960-1127 A.D.) courts.

Among the five great kilns of the Song Dynasty, three of which were devoted to making celadon, which were the Imperial, Ru and Ge kilns. However, each kiln style had its distinctive celadon colors which set them apart. The Ru kiln mostly produced celadon that were sky blue and glue-grey; the Imperial and Ge kilns have more similar colors, where the glazes can be light greenish blue, moon white, glossy gray, yellow green and so on.

Of all the celadon of the Song Dynasty, Jingdezhen's Qingbai, or blue and white porcelain, was the most unique. With thin and refined body, its decorative patterns sometimes cast projections when light strikes through them. The glaze was clear and sparkling, making Qingbai porcelain win over other porcelain products for its purity and refinement. The decorative motifs on Qingbai were exquisite, as carved, painted, imprinted and embossed sculpture images were expertly applied. It has become a prestigious brand and representative of Song Dynasty porcelain wares. Under its influence, many kilns around Fujian, Guangdong, Sichuan, Zhejiang, Anhui, Hubei, Yunnan, Guangxi and other provinces all began to imitate and produce Qingbai, eventually establishing a family of Qingbai kilns in China. Since Qingbai porcelain was an attempt to recreate the splendor of green-white jade ware, thus its glaze color fell between green and white. Its name was the general term representing a whole family of porcelains where white was found within green and vice versa.

Chinese celadon after the Song Dynasty kept on a course of development. However, by the Yuan Dynasty, a new trend in Chinese ceramics began as more folk elements were adopted into the craft. The simplistic and clean look began to give way to brightly colored and decorated wares. People no longer wanted celadon that were as pure and clear as jade and with only a single layer of glaze. Instead, they turn to colored porcelain with its many illustrated surfaces with stories and splendid imagery.

Chapter **6**

The One-of-a-Kind
Tri-Colored Pottery

Chinese Ceramics

Sancai, or tri-colored pottery, was the magnificent flagship ceramic ware of the Tang Dynasty, as it held not only a unique style but a special function. During an archeological dig at the beginning of the 20th century, people uncovered, near an ancient tomb at Luoyang in Henan Province, large quantities Tang-styled, tri-colored pottery made in the Ming Dynasty. Its one of a kind artistic expression was known to the world once again.

Women riding horse, Tang-style tri-colored pottery.

The tri-colored pottery was based on and as an improvement of the lead-glaze pottery of the Han Dynasty. It had bodies made of white pottery clay and covered in low-temperature glaze which contained lead. The glaze itself was mixed with iron, copper, manganese, cobalt and other metals as coloring, and then fired at temperatures between 750 to 800 degrees Celsius. The so called "tri-color" really pertains to multiple colors, including green, yellow, burnt ochre, red, white, blue, black and more. Some colors were applied singularly while others were applied as mixtures. Before applying glaze, a layer of dressing clay was used, followed by layer after layer of colored glaze in order to realize the intended effect. Some tri-colored pottery adopted traditional decorative styles such as impression, appliqué, engravings, embossed sculpture and so on. The tri-colored pottery ingeniously conveyed lavish effects and sometimes vivid stories.

Some Tang-style tri-colored (Tang Sancai) potteries sported gold outlines, which appeared particularly extravagant. Among the excavated works from tombs of Tang Dynasty imperial members, this golden outline effect was especially striking. The

Camel sculpture in the Tang tri-color pottery style.

Merchant and camel sculpture in the Tang tri-color pottery style.

Beijing Palace Museum and Shaanxi Museum, respectively house the tri-colored camel figurine and sculpture of man playing instrument on camel back, which are both priceless collection pieces, modeled in the realistic style. The camel figurines are about 1 meter tall, depicted in either a marching pose or upright standing posture, appearing sumptuous and in grand spirit. The firing and modeling are excellent on both pieces. These double-humped camels, the models for which the sculptures were based, often traversed the Silk Road in the Tang Dynasty and were of a Central Asia origin. More than just a mode of transportation, with their "exotic" appearances, these camels were loved by all people in China during its time. It serves as an indication as to how active and frequent commercial activities and artistic performances were back in the old days. Tri-colored pottery from the Tang Dynasty was a tremendous breakthrough from the monotony, crudeness and rigid styling of the single-colored, glazed pottery. With its realistic and romantic presentation (e.g. figures, animals, tomb beasts), Tang Sancai tells of the prosperous times when nationalities and cultures converged and foreign

Sancai (tri-colored) phoenix-headed pottery vase.

Sancai (tri-colored) ewer with leave-shaped opening.

Tang Dynasty ewer of foreign form and design, which was heavily influenced by Persian cultures, with characteristics of the Sasanian silver ewer.

exchanges were frequent.

Findings of buried Tang-style tri-colored pottery were mostly concentrated around Xi'an and Luoyang, both northern Chinese cities. From excavations of kiln sites, the Gong County in Henan, Xing Kilns in Hebei and Yaozhou kilns of Shaanxi were the centers of production. In the south, areas such as Changsha and Wuhan had Tang mausoleums that unveiled works of tri-colored pottery. What's special was that these potteries had very well preserved glazes, smooth and glistening. It also had very strong and interesting local styling, an indications that they may very well have been produced at kilns nearby. Aside from the type of tri-colored pottery that were used as burial objects, there were also many vessels made for daily use, such as jars, kettles, lamps, dishes, bowls and so forth.

Tri-colored pottery was immensely popular during the height of the Tang Dynasty. It was sold domestically as well as exported to far away countries. After the late-Tang period, tri-colored pottery production dwindled; the works produced were also not as exquisite and high quality as those of the prime Tang period. By the Five Dynasties Period, tri-colored pottery was no longer produced. However, its impact on colored pottery and porcelain of later periods were immense. Even though its glory was short lived, Tang Sancai is still a most favored artifact for people today.

Chapter 7

The Age of Porcelain and the Five Great Kilns

"The Song Dynasty rose up in 960 A.D.; China seemingly entered a modern age when a kind of material culture began. The circulation of hard currency was more universalized compared to previous dynasties. Inventions such as gunpowder, ancient flame throwers, the mariner's compass used in maritime navigation, astronomical clock, blast furnace, hydraulic spinning machine, the use of watertight chest in shipbuilding and so on, all appeared during the Song Dynasty. During the 11th and 12th centuries, the living standards in major Chinese cities show no inferiority when compared to any other city in the world." These were the words of renowned contemporary historian Ray Huang in his book *The Grand History of China*, which presented Song Dynasty features in all its glory.

Without a doubt, the Song Dynasty was an important segment in ancient Chinese history. There were two stages, the Northern Song and Southern Song periods, spanning a total of 320 years. Regardless of material or spiritual culture, all flourished and expanded upon the foundations of the Tang Dynasty, and exceeding those of the Tang on a general scope.

Speaking of the prosperous commercial scenes of the Song Dynasty, people often connect it in their minds with a great painting — Upriver Scenes During the Bright and Pure Festival by Northern Song artist Zhang Zeduan. This painting on a scroll 18 feet-long depicts the heyday of the then capital city of Bianliang, from the countryside to busy urban areas. Each section of the scroll reflects a different time of day. The far right section shows farmers driving donkeys hauling baskets full of vegetables to the market; the time is early morning as the trees are enshrouded in morning mist. The left side is showing a performance troupe answering a curtain call; the time is of dusk and the peddlers after a hard day's work are gathering up leftover supplies, ready to return home. A total of over 500 people are depicted in the painting, each with different personalities, dress and going by their own routines. There are city gates, street crossings, large streets and small alleyways; there are people peddling on the street sides, as well as three-story tall shops, inns, all types of restaurants, teahouses and food shops all over the city. There is an arch bridge in the middle of the city connecting both banks of the Bian River, in

which are about two dozen tour and merchant boats. In terms of material living, 12th century China was undoubtedly leading the rest of the world.

Record has it that at the end of the Northern Song Dynasty, in the city of Kaifeng, "city dwellers often shop for food or dine at restaurants, and do not grow their own crops;" "the night market ends around midnight and reopens at the break of dawn; at the busiest places, the shops never close;" "In the winter months, despite wind, snow and rain, the night market is alive and well." Even at small towns or main traffic pivots, taverns and teahouses were readily available. Country and city inns also provided dining services. People of the Song Dynasty mostly had three meals per day. The old tradition of sitting on mats on the floor has totally changed. The culinary techniques of the Song Dynasty was very much like the cooking of the Chinese in the present day, using water, oil and all sorts of sauces to boil, steam, stir-fry, deep fry, fry, dice and braise, and roast their foods. People of the upper social classes in the Song Dynasty held banquets with lavish settings, as extravagant and wasteful conduct was actually the prevailing social trend. In the capital city of the Southern Song Dynasty, the commissions for chefs of the highest class were not affordable to even the prefecture government. It was obvious just how costly classy banquets could be. Tea and spirits were the most important drinks of the Song people; even for people of the lowest social ranks, tea was a crucial tool for socializing. Drinking alcohol was prevalent in all social classes, as many nobilities and wealthy merchants have self-made liquor stored in their homes. The high development of the food and beverage industry required large quantities of vessels for day to day use. Song liquors were sold in flasks; when brewing or drinking tea, different tea ware was called for; and banquets hired servants specifically to attend to the dining utensils. All the above factors undoubtedly helped to advance Song Dynasty porcelain industry very rapidly.

On the aesthetic side, the "rejuvenation of Confucianism" had profound impact on Song porcelain. The Song emperor encouraged the practice of nurturing top talents. Thus there were a group of influential philosophers and thinkers born from the scholar-officials in the Imperial government. New concepts sprung

Dragon-handled and cock-headed white pottery, H 27.4 cm, Dia. at mouth 5.9 cm, Dia. at waist 11.5 cm, Dia. at foot 7.1 cm, weight 0.8 kg. Sui Dynasty. The National Museum of China.

up everywhere as Confucian ethics were juxtaposed upon Buddhist and Daoist views of the universe. The Song people believed the motions of the universe contained infinite cause-and-effect relationships. People's doings should be in accordance with the laws of nature, which they referred to as "heavenly justice." A kind of self-awareness was thus gradually promulgated throughout the society of the scholar-officials – "the scholars shall carry the worries of the world before the people, and shall feel the joy in the world after the people." They shouldered the responsibilities of the country as their own duty; this has become the spirit of their era, as to strengthen righteousness and firm attitudes in later Chinese Confucianists. In regards to aesthetics, they were focused upon the intangible life experiences, launching a purely spiritual search in nature. Therefore, the aesthetic ideal of the Song Dynasty returned to the expression of natural order, finding rhythm from within stillness and silence; this was transcending the mere satisfaction of people's senses. Synthetic decorations were no longer the preferred style; instead, taste for the natural and simplistic was of the highest standard. This kind of aesthetic preference was especially apparent in Song Dynasty porcelain ware.

Great inventions such as gunpowder, the mariner's compass and movable type printing signified a time of rapid breakthroughs in science and technology. The porcelain craft industry, as it was closely related to technology, entered the "age of porcelain." Newly established kilns sprouted up from all parts of the country. Regardless of celadon, white porcelain, black porcelain or overglazed or underglazed colored porcelain, the craftsmanship improved by a great deal. There were many innovative new methods in modeling, decorative images, body and glaze. Song Dynasty porcelain, with its simplistic and elegant designs, captivating colors and an infinitely varied crystallization and crackling patterns, was famed throughout the world. The so-called "Five Great Kilns" including Ding, Ru, Imperial, Ge and Jun kilns were the cream of the crop.

Ding Kilns

Production sites of Ding kilns were found in present day Quyang County, Hebei Province. Quyang County back in the Song Dynasty was within the Dingzhou region, hence the name Ding kilns. The history of the Ding kilns can be traced back based on unearthed specimens. There were white porcelains being made here as early as the Tang Dynasty; by the Five Dynasties Period, the porcelain business here was already booming. After the Northern Song Dynasty, Ding kilns were famous for its off-white glazes and exquisite engravings, etchings, and imprinted patterns on porcelain. Porcelain kilns from other areas all strove to imitate Ding porcelain, which became the standard of white porcelain in China. Aside from white porcelain, the Ding kilns also produced black, crimson, and green glazed porcelain. Its technology and varieties in glaze colors were astonishing.

Early Ding porcelain was single colored with little or no decoration; by late-Northern Song Dynasty however, there would be exquisite patterns on porcelain wares, which were engraved, etched or imprinted. The patterns were precisely laid out, with a clear sense of sections and layers; lines were clear and organized into loose and dense areas. Popular motifs included water waves, swimming fish, land animals, birds, flowers, and playful children. Peonies, lotuses, and pomegranates and so on were the most common floral motifs. Engraved floral décor was the principal way of ornamentation in early Song porcelain. Once the technique caught on, it was combined with comb-etched images as another form of ornamentation. For example, at the center part of a flare-lip dish, the image of a flower was first carved, then with a fine-toothed comb, the area within the outlines of the leaves were comb-etched, leaving parallel lines that represent veins of the leaves. The most popular motifs done in this technique were the lotus, peony and so on. Engravings usually relied on bamboo chips and knives, while comb-etchings relied on a tool similar in shape to a comb to leave orderly patterns on the body. The combined result was commonly referred to as "bamboo outlines with brushed patterns," with lines that were tidy and natural. Imprinted patterns on Ding porcelain first appeared in mid-Northern Song Dynasty, and matured late in the dynasty. The patterned décor was often place on the insides of plates and bowls. To make imprinted patterns, it would require a mold with engraved patterns, which is pressed onto the not yet dried surface of the clay body. Most often, the imprinted image would be a positive image and would have added thickness and can create a very special effect of depth when light strikes the object. The motifs and designs were normally borrowed from silk tapestry or gold and silverware produced in the Dingzhou area. Therefore, imprinted motifs on Ding porcelain have appeared to be mature in style right from the start, with very high artistic merits. It had quite an effect on imprinted designs of latter generations.

The Song Dynasty Ding kilns produced vessels such as bowls,

Ding kiln gui *with animal-shaped handles and tile patterns. Northern Song Dynasty. Collection of the Changfound Museum, Taipei, China.*

Toddler-shaped porcelain pillow. Song Dynasty, L 40 cm, W 14 cm, H 18.3 cm. The Palace Museum, Beijing.

Maroon pot with gold painting. H 18.1 cm, Dia. 9.1 cm at mouth. Ding Kiln. Northern Song Dynasty. Collection of the Anhui Provincial Museum. It has a thin body in brown glaze with gold and colored patterns.

dishes, jars, cups, cases, vases, and pots, all for daily use. Vessels such as bowls with their large mouths and thinly cast bodies, needed to be overturned when fired in order to avoid deformation. Therefore at the mouth, there was the absence of glaze which felt quite astringent. High class items often have copper, gold or silver rims at the mouths. Rare items were the round-bottomed jars and baby-shaped pillows with forms that were realistic and cuddly. From today's surviving examples of Ding kilns' quality works, people have found especially valuable pieces which contained inscriptions, imprinted writing or handwritings.

Among the five great kilns of the Song Dynasty, only the Ding kilns produced white porcelain, and it was quite famous during its time. It was for a time offered as tribute to the imperial families, but was then discontinued for an unclear cause. The official given reason was that ding porcelain had unglazed parts. This was because Ding porcelain was produced through upside-down firing, and had no glaze at its mouth. However, Ding porcelain often had extensive gold, silver and copper edged around the unglazed rim. Therefore, some people believe that the real reason for discontinuing imperial use of Ding porcelain was not because of the unglazed areas. Instead, it was attributed to the aesthetic preferences of its times. The white of the Ding porcelain was turbid, opaque and bland. In order to counter such a drawback, most Ding wares were decorated with imprinted or engraved patterns. When compared to porcelain of the Ge, Imperial, Ru and Jun kilns, Ding porcelain contained more synthetic features, which fell short of achieving the ideals of natural and subtle beauty in the Song Dynasty. For this reason, Ding porcelain did not quite capture the interest of the literati class, and may have been considered objects of somewhat vulgar taste and style.

Ru Kilns

The Ru kilns have been oft mentioned by the writings of the literati. However, it was not until 1987 that a kiln site was actually discovered in a monastery that fired porcelain for the imperial government. The Ru kilns produced porcelain for the court for only a short twenty some years; the rest of the time was devoted

Tri-pod writing-brush washbasin, H 3.6 cm, Dia. 18.3 cm at mouth. Ru kiln. Collection of the Palace Museum, Beijing.

to porcelain ware for average citizen use. Therefore, porcelains made by the Ru kilns for the imperial court known today are few and rare piece of treasure (less than 100 specimens in existence today). Due to its rarity, imperial Ru wares were sometimes hailed during the Ming and Qing Dynasties as the best of the Song kilns.

According to the book *About Ceramics* from the Qing Dynasty, "Ru kilns were originally producers of celadon." Archeological digs further proved that sky-blue celadon, black porcelain, celadon, and Song tri-colored ware existed during the same time. The Ru celadon wares in the permanent collections of the Beijing Palace Museum, Shanghai Museum and Tianjin Museum all had glazes of a light sky blue color. Some were relatively darker and some were a bit subtler; all were smooth with restrained luster. There were fine and dense crackles that resembled crackling of ice. The Chinese slang for this effect was "crab claw veins."

When the Ru kilns fired celadon, the ware was first fired in oxidation flame, then in reduction flame. The temperature was kept at relatively low levels (1,125 to 1,225 degrees Celsius), followed by a period of natural cool down so as to cause crystallization in the glaze. The rich amounts of crystals covered more than half of the glazed area. Sparse air bubbles also formed. Since Ru celadon experienced good crystallization during the firing process, its glazed surfaces not only showed a sky-blue color, a jade-like turbidity was also present.

The sizes of most Ru porcelain vessels were usually rather small, none exceeded 30 cm in height; most were around 20 cm or so. The sizes of dishes, writing-brush basin, plates and other round wares were from 10 to 16 cm in diameter at the mouths. Those over 20 cm were very rare. The bodies of Ru porcelain were all quite thin and grayish in color. Round vessels such as plates and bowls were glazed in entirety, not exposing any areas of the body. Since these porcelains were fired while on extremely thin supporting stands, the back sides of most Ru wares had three to five very small burn marks. The ancients described these marks as "sesame-sized."

Imperial Kilns

The Song imperial kilns were centralized in two locations; at the former capital city of Bianjing (present day Kaifeng city) during the Northern Song Dynasty, and later at the city of Hangzhou in the Southern Song Dynasty after the regime moved southward. The Northern Song Imperial kilns produced celadon, but with various shades and luster in the glaze. The glaze colors included light greenish blue, moon white, glossy gray and yellow-green. Though the colors were different, they all contained the common element of green or blue-green, and its beauty was heightened by the use of different colored bodies. The bodies can be blackish gray, dark gray,

Statue of the Guanyin Bodhisattva, H 19.1 cm, Dehua Kiln.
Ming Dynasty. Collection of the Chongqing Museum.

light gray or earth yellow, and when coated in glaze, produced different greens and blues. Since the body colors were quite deep, it conveyed a sense of unfathomable sophistication; it was perhaps what the literati sought for during that time.

The bodies most often used for Imperial wares contained rather high concentrations of iron, producing an effect called "purple mouth and iron feet." At the mouth of the vessel, the glaze was thin, revealing the ground underneath and thus the purplish color; the feet had no glaze at all, showing the iron rich body, which turned black after being fired. Imperial porcelain also borrowed from Ru kiln's technique of decorating the porcelain with crackles, which gave the vessel extra pizzazz in glaze color as well as an antiqueness and sophistication. This kind of beauty occurred naturally through the glazing process and changes in technology, and was in accord with Song Dynasty ideologies.

Historical records describe that the Imperial kilns of the Southern Song Dynasty were "located at the foot of Mount Phoenix." At the described location, tons of shards from porcelain wares and kiln equipment were discovered, but the actual ruins of the kilns were never discovered. It was not until September of 1996 that someone unintentionally discovered the Tiger Cave kiln, a site near the ruins of the Southern

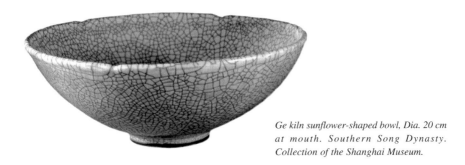

Ge kiln sunflower-shaped bowl, Dia. 20 cm at mouth. Southern Song Dynasty. Collection of the Shanghai Museum.

Song imperial city near Mount Phoenix. The kiln site's location was exactly where the Imperial *Xiuneisi* was located. Among the large amounts of porcelain fragments, inscriptions in brown coloring that read *"Xiuneisi"* or "Imperial Kiln" were found underneath glazed porcelain fragments that used to be the base parts of vessels. In an excavation by the Hangzhou Cultural Relic and Archeology Institute that followed, more Imperial ware fragments and kiln tools were uncovered. A second Imperial kiln was built during the Southern Song Dynasty, named Jiaotan Imperial kiln. Its ruins remain today at the southern suburbs of Hangzhou City.

Imperial porcelain of the Southern Song excelled in glaze color, the crackling effect of the glaze and form of the vessels. They were presented in modest simplicity, yet elegant. The glazing effect made it feel moist and smooth as if jade. Minimal decorations were used. Aside from the commonly seen plant and animal motifs, there were also all types of parallel lines, the eight trigrams, cloud and thunder, geometric, rings, dots and so on. Techniques of decoration included engravings, mold imprints, relief, sculpturing, pierced patterns, pierced sculptures and more. Engraving was mostly used on bowls, dishes and other containers for daily use. Mold imprints were more widely adopted by the full range of vessels. Embossed sculptures were mostly used for vases, kettles, stoves and wine vessels, which were retro styled vessels. Pierced sculpture was for decorating lids, pedestals and stoves. With the growing number of ways of decoration and improvements in porcelain firing techniques, as well as for a multitude of crafting tools, the quality of Southern Song Imperial kilns were top notch. It is clear that strong emphasis was placed on the development of Imperial kilns in the Southern Song Dynasty.

Fenqing gui-*type stove. Imperial kiln. Southern Song Dynasty. Collection of the Palace Museum of Taipei, China.

Ge Kilns

The Ge kilns had always been a mystery in the history of ceramics. Although authentic Ge porcelain wares are on display in the Beijing Palace Museum, Shanghai Museum and the Palace Museum of Taipei and so on, there is no surviving documentation from the Song Dynasty, nor had any kiln sites ever been identified.

From existing Ge ware, we see all kinds of stoves, vases and dishes, including tripod cauldrons, cauldrons with fish-shaped handles, cauldron with glazed feet and double handles, cylindrical vases, thin-necked urns, bent bodied plates and so on, mostly imitating the designs of ritualistic bronze ware and were intended for court use. Thus it had common elements with Ru and Imperial kilns but was very different from porcelain for the common people.

The most distinguished feature of Ge porcelain ware would be its crackling patterns. The surface of the glaze displays natural patterns such as ice-crackles, fine crackles, or fish egg crackles and so forth.. The areas enclosed within the cracks can vary from the size of large chunks of ice to speckles as small as fish eggs. The actual crackle lines also vary in width and can be filled in with different colors such as black, gold or red. This effect is sometimes referred to as "gold and iron threads." The crackling in the glaze is caused by differences in the degree of expansion of various parts of the glaze. This was originally an imperfection in technology, but was taken advantage of by porcelain artisans and made into added aesthetic element.

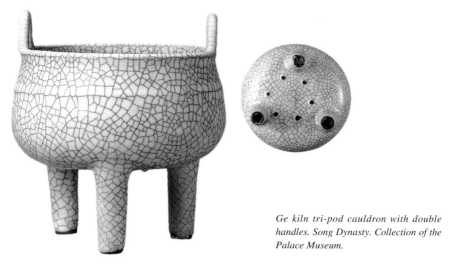

Ge kiln tri-pod cauldron with double handles. Song Dynasty. Collection of the Palace Museum.

Jun Kilns

The Jun kilns were based in Henan Province and had locations throughout its Yu County. As of today, over 100 kiln sites have been discovered. Some of which specially produced porcelain ware for the imperial courts, with a history that dated back to the Tang Dynasty; its most flourishing period was during the Song Dynasty. The unique feature of Jun porcelain lied with its special turbid glaze, which contained low concentrates of copper oxide. If we consider iron oxide the coloring agents for celadon and black porcelain, then Jun porcelain gained its wonderful hues from copper oxide. Copper turns green in oxidation fire and red instead in reduction atmosphere. Due to the small traces of copper oxide in Jun porcelain glaze, its color was often green infused

*Jizhou kiln porcelain vase with spiral
cloud patterns. Song Dynasty.*

with violet, as if the rosy clouds during sunset. Even the blue contained in Jun porcelain was different from the usual celadon; it was a blue with a milky tone. The successful creation of Jun porcelain was a great achievement by the craftsmen of the Song Dynasty. Its mysterious and unpredictable colors have gained the love of the people during its time, making the Jun kilns one of the most famous around.

By using copper oxides as the pigment, the Jun kilns successfully produced copper-red glaze in a reduction fire. This was a breakthrough in the technology of ceramics. Adding copper oxide as coloring agent was a rather difficult task, as the chemical components in the basic glaze, the temperature and atmosphere were all very sensitive factors. Even the smallest bit of deviation from the requirements would have resulted in an undesirable shade of red. Another distinguishing feature of Jun porcelain glaze would be the pattern referred to as "earthworm crawling in the mud." It appeared as if the trails left in the soil by earthworms. This was a result of the glaze being particularly thick in Jun ware. When in the process of baking, under low temperatures, the glaze began to chap. When the temperature was raised, glaze that had not congealed flowed back into the crackled creases. Just as the crackle glaze, this defect in firing technology turned into a kind of rich and unique decorative language. There is a saying that no two pieces of Jun porcelain are identical, which means that even porcelain born of the same kiln are somewhat different, as most of the coloring is done through a natural process; people have little control over the glaze color. However, this type of natural formation was the highest ideal in aesthetics at the time.

Jun porcelain vessels such as flower pots, cauldrons, writing-brush washbasins and more; all modeled after ancient bronze vessels used for rituals. Thus Jun porcelain appeared retrospective and stately, with the most meticulous attention to detail. There were similarities between Jun porcelain and those of the Imperial, Ru and other kilns of the same time period, because they were all intended for serving the courts. Flowers and floral patterns were the fashionable form of decoration for porcelain at this time. However, Jun porcelain used not patterned

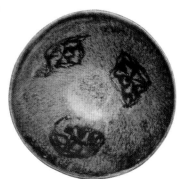

Rhombic-lined paper-cuts on rabbit fluff ground, Song Dynasty.

decorations but the vessels themselves came in the shapes of flowers. Commonly seen were toilet cases, flowerpots, flat bowls and writing-brush washbasins in the shape of Chinese crabapple flowers; Flowerpots and pot bases in the shape of lotuses; as well as pot bases made to resemble sunflowers. It was a truly unique feature of the Jun kilns.

Of the five aforementioned great kilns of the Song Dynasty, aside from Ding porcelain which had engraved or imprinted patterns as decorations, the other kilns all produced purely non-decorated porcelain. Of course this absence of ornamentation did not equal to being bland, rather it was reliance on natural formation. The Ge, Imperial and Ru kilns all produced celadon, and all three utilized crackle glaze as a form of decoration. The crackle glaze was caused by different degrees of contraction at different parts of the glaze. Thus when fired, the surface of the glaze would begin to chap. This may originally have been an imperfection of the firing technology. However, porcelain artisans were able to take advantage of this defect and made it a naturally formed decorative element.

Jun Kiln flowerpot in rosy purple glaze, Northern Song Dynasty. Collection of the Palace Museum, Beijing.

In the annals of history, there were many kilns that were less often mentioned and came to be judged as less important. However, they also produced great porcelain wares, as the Song Dynasty was a time when masterpiece porcelain ware emerged in an endless stream. Aside from the kilns already discussed, there were also the Ying celadon of the town of Jingdezhen; celadon of the Longquan kilns; the Tuhao and Youdi porcelains from the Jian kilns and much more. All these famous porcelain embodied the aesthetic principles advocated by high society during their times. In addition, Cizhou kilns, Jizhou kilns, Yaozhou kilns and other commoner's kilns, with locations throughout China, produced porcelain that had vivid and unique styles and body, capturing the eyes of collectors and connoisseurs both domestic and abroad. For example, the porcelain-making technology of Cizhou kilns were spread to many parts of China, and even influenced Korea, Japan, Thailand, Vietnam and other countries, who produced similar porcelain wares.

Jun kiln zun *in indigo blue glaze. Northern Song Dynasty. Collection of the China National Museum.*

Chapter **8**

Qinghua Porcelain with Chinese Ink and Wash

The fine art style in Western Asia influenced the Chinese Qinghua porcelain in glaze colors and patterns.

Speaking of the contributions of the "porcelain capital" – Jingdezhen to Chinese ceramics, we must start with the Qinghua porcelain of the Yuan Dynasty. There were other areas that produced Qinghua in the Yuan Dynasty, such as Jiangshan of Zhejiang Province, Jianshui and Yuxi of Yunnan Province. However, none of them came even close to the sheer quality, volume and aesthetic value of Jingdezhen Qinghua. Qinghua porcelain was a kind of underglaze colored porcelain. It relied on natural cobalt minerals as coloring, painting imagery and motifs on top of the clay body with Chinese calligraphy brush. Then with the application of a transparent glaze, it was fired a single time

Qinghua jar with lid and floral spread decorations. Hongwu period, Ming Dynasty.

under high temperatures. Its was first created in Gong County, Henan Province in the Tang Dynasty, and continued to be produced through the Song Dynasty. By the Yuan Dynasty, the art had attained a level of maturity. Its colors were refined and elegant, capturing the gracefulness of traditional Chinese ink and wash paintings. Starting with the Yuan and through the Ming and Qing Dynasties, regardless of Imperial kilns or commoner's kilns, the Qinghua was a most popular product. The Qinghua was also the colored porcelain product with artistic style that was most representative of the Chinese. It also started with Qinghua

Qinghua Yuhuchun vase with design of
mandarin ducks frolicking in water.
Yuan Dynasty.

porcelain in the Yuan Dynasty, as single-colored Chinese porcelain began to be replaced by porcelain ware with colored decorations.

There were several reasons for the maturing of Qinghua porcelain in the Yuan Dynasty. Prior to that time, Jingdezhen's porcelain wares from porcelain stones were comparatively soft, with maturing temperatures at 1,200 degrees Celsius. The newly discovered Kaolin was then mixed with porcelain stone as the raw material. The compound material raised maturing temperatures to 1,300 degrees Celsius, also improving hardness and rigidity in the porcelain body. In addition, higher aluminum content in Kaolin made the porcelain whiter in color, an improvement in body that laid the foundation for the creation of Qinghua. Jingdezhen produced no colored porcelain in the Tang and Song Dynasties. The Qingbai, or blue and white, porcelain of the Song Dynasty was only added artistic treatment to the original color of the porcelain. However, with paintings and illustrations as the foremost decorative method, the Qinghua required a manual painting technique never before used in Jingdezhen. Amidst the turbulence of the war between the Song Chinese and the Yuan Mongolians, a great influx of ceramic artisans from the Cizhou kilns of northern China found its way to Jingdezhen; these people possessed this kind of painting skills. Soon after, imprinted, painted and engraved images began to appear on the glistening white surfaces of porcelain ware. It was the new prevalence in Yuan Dynasty porcelain-making. Aside from provisions for the daily consumption and use of the Chinese, the need for porcelain supply in overseas trade also stimulated the porcelain industry in the Yuan Dynasty.

The Yuan Dynasty, ruled by the Mongols, spanned across Europe and Asia, which built the grounds for a broad and extensive market for the commercial and handicraft industries. Especially in the early parts of the Yuan Dynasty, there were once protective measures implemented for export goods. The shipbuilding industry, intimately tied in with overseas trading, was already a booming business by the Northern Song Dynasty. There were increased demands from abroad for Chinese porcelain and silk products every year, including the areas of East Asia, Central Asia, West Asia, Southeast Asia, East Africa, North Africa, and West Africa and so on. In fact, the ceramics industry of West Asia, since the 10th century, has never stopped production of underglaze colored ware, especially the Qinghua. Today, in the Freer

Qinghua Meiping vase with lid and peony scroll patterns. Yuan Dynasty. Collection of the Ge Family Tianminlou Foundation of Hong Kong.

*Qinghua vase with white dragon in seawater
design. Imperial Family kiln of Jingdezhen.
Xuande period, Ming Dynasty.*

Gallery of Art in Washington D.C. are 14th century Qinghua bowls with underglaze
paintings in blue, green and white; all were made in Iran. However, due to the rather
poor quality of the raw material used for the body and glaze in the Middle East, and
with a lower maturing temperature, its was never able achieve the quality of Chinese
Qinghua porcelain.

Topkapi Palace in Turkey houses 13,508 pieces of Chinese porcelain, 40 of which
are Qinghua. It is considered the largest and finest collection of Yuan Dynasty Qinghua

Qinghua dish with floral and fruit spread patterns on yellow ground. Zhengde period, Ming Dynasty. Collection of the Palace Museum.

anywhere in the world. The collection includes many Yuan Qinghua specimens such
as large dishes, bowls, bottle gourd, octagon Meiping vases and so on. Dense patterns
adorn the entire bodies of the vessel, not leaving any blank areas of the ground;
something rarely seen in domestic Chinese vessels. The illustrations are exquisite
and with a sense of depth; the colors are compelling with uniform application. Overall,
these motifs and the brightness of the Qinghua colors can be considered the finest in
the world, surpassing the quality Chinese domestic Qinghua by far. Many pieces of
this collection are one of a kind: the largest polygonal dish in the world with a diameter
of 41.5 cm, sports white patterns on blue ground, showing the mystical animal – Kylin
and two phoenixes; the bottle gourd with peony motifs, 70 cm tall, is also the only one
of its kind in the world; another pair of polygonal calabash are the tallest in the world,
and many more. Why is it that the most exquisite pieces of Yuan Dynasty Qinghua are
not in China, but instead rest in the palace of an exotic land? This is evidence of a
prosperous time in the history of Sino-foreign cultural and commercial exchanges. These
porcelain wares were not made for the use or consumption by Chinese, instead were

custom made for the Islamic nations. Through the Silk Road, Chinese porcelain found its way to Central and West Asia, and was loved by the royalties of the Ottoman Empire; it was the symbol of fashion and luxury for their times. In order to coincide their religious beliefs with functional items, West Asian merchants brought with them cobalt coloring and drawings of their desired products to Jingdezhen of China, and placed their orders directly. These porcelain wares were considered further processing of supplied material, and were tailored for the customs in Islamic cultures; thus it was rarely seen in China. It is highly probable that West Asian artisans joined the design and making of Yuan Dynasty Qinghua. The area named Samarra in present day Iraq, rich in cobalt, was confirmed the supplying region for the blue underglaze coloring called "Sumali-Qing" used in Yuan Dynasty Qinghua porcelain. Through large amounts of material evidence and records of history, it was further confirmed that from the 13th to mid-15th century, there were merchants, monks and missionaries from Persia, Syria and other places, who traversed the land and sea Silk Routes and brought to China all kinds of trade goods, handicrafts, spices and cobalt blue, a coloring produced in Islamic nations. In return, they brought back to their own countries Qinghua porcelain as well as other Chinese handicraft goods. The principal port of China at the time was Quanzhou, a gathering place for wealthy Muslim merchants. They purchased Qinghua porcelain in mass quantities and resold them to Iran, Syria, Lebanon, Turkey, Italy, Egypt, Kenya, Tanzania and others countries. As a result, Jingdezhen's artisans not only received the coloring agent from which spurred Yuan Dynasty Qinghua, they also had a market so big that they never imagined possible. Fine china ware became the symbol of China,

Club-shaped Qinghua vase with figure, frontal and rear views. Commoner's kiln. Kangxi period, Qing Dynasty. Collection of the Palace Museum.

spread along the land and maritime Silk Routes to other corners of the world in all directions. It is easy to see the influences it had on porcelain manufacturing in other countries of the world.

Since Yuan Qinghua was heavily targeted at export, there are many examples of such export ware still preserved in other countries today. In preliminary count, there are more than 300 specimens of Yuan Qinghua in existence today, preserved both in China and in overseas countries. The overseas pieces add up to about 110, mainly housed in Turkey, Iran and so forth; Chinese domestic collections are around 200 pieces, mostly archeological findings around China after 1949. These domestic pieces are mostly parts of the collections at Beijing Palace Museum, Beijing Capital Museum, Shanghai museum and others. In the Ardebil Shrine of Iran, great collection of Chinese porcelain can be found. Aside from Longquan celadon of the Southern Song and Yuan Dynasties, white porcelain of southern China, imperial porcelain of the Privy Council and blue glazed porcelain of the Yuan Dynasty, there is another 37 valuable pieces of Qinghua from the Yuan Dynasty. In the northwestern part of Iran, among the collections of the Azerbaijan Museum in Tabriz, are also Qinghua porcelain and underglazed red porcelain. Among which are large Qinghua dishes, Meiping vases and bowls of the late Ming Dynasty, all are fine specimens of extraordinary splendor. In Istanbul, Turkey, an internationally renowned museum is well known to house large collections of Chinese porcelain.

Furthermore, more Qinghua porcelain vessels or fragments were found in places such as Fustat in Egypt, along the Red Sea in Sudan, on the Island of Barain in the Persian Gulf, and East African countries such as Somali, Kenya, Tanzania and so on. In recent years, more Yuan Dynasty Qinghua was discovered in Japan, Thailand and the Philippines. Especially in the Philippines, large jars and bowls were discovered, such as Qinghua jars with quadruple handles sporting the double dragon motif. These Qinghua porcelains contain designs of flowers and birds, birds and wild animals, flowers and herbage, floral scrolls and geometric designs and so on. They were quite different from the early Qinghua wares seen in Japan. One of which was a small jar

Unearthed large Qinghua crock with dragon motifs. Both belly depth and diameter of around 70 cm. Imperial Family kiln of Jingdezhen. Jiajing period, Ming Dynasty.

Qinghua vase with cloud and dragon motif and dual elephant-shaped handles. Yuan Dynasty. Collection of the Percival David Foundation of Chinese Art, University of London, U.K.

with double handles with Chrysanthemum image; its form and decorative images was exactly the same as porcelain uncovered from Yahutian Kilns in Jingdezhen, which belonged to the products of late-Yuan Dynasty. Later, when the imperial ambassador (eunuch) Zheng He sailed seven times on long journeys west, not only were maritime trade routes established between China and other countries, he also brought great quantities of magnificent Qinghua porcelain to these far away lands.

Even though the production of Qinghua porcelain in the Yuan Dynasty was already a success, due to limited historical records, evidences that could give affirmative dating were lacking. Thus there was a few hundred years of uncertain history and understanding for the art of Qinghua porcelain. Even as recent as half a century ago, the existence of Yuan Dynasty Qinghua in China was still a topic of debate.

The story of the discovery of Yuan Dynasty Qinghua began with one such work that found its way to Britain. Around the 20's to the 30's of the twentieth century, British man R.L. Hobson first disclosed the fact that among the Chinese Qinghua porcelain collections of the Percival David Foundation was a pair of identical vases with duo elephant-shaped handles, decorated with the image of the dragon and phoenix. The vases were 63.6 cm tall, with motifs including chrysanthemums scroll patterns, palm leaves, lotuses scroll motifs, flying phoenix, heavenly dragon swimming in the seas motif, peony scroll motifs, miscellaneous treasures and lotus petal patterns, layer after layer. The neck of the vases had a lengthy inscription written in Qinghua coloring, describing the exact time and place that the vessel was bestowed as a gift of good luck and the people involved in the process. The date marked was of the 11th year of the Zhizheng period (1351 A.D.), which was under the reign of the last Yuan Emperor, Huizong. Before the Yuan Dynasty, Chinese porcelain did not have the custom of marking the year and place of production on porcelain ware. Therefore, the discovery of such a special piece of Qinghua held unprecedented importance; it was the first time that people of the world were aware of Yuan Dynasty Qinghua porcelain, made in Jingdezhen.

The report by Hobson was overly simple and lacked

Qinghua dish with image of elegant ladies. Kangxi period, Qing Dynasty. Collection of the Palace Museum.

convincing evidence, thus it id not gain the attention of the academic world. It was not until the 50's of the twentieth century, when American scholar Dr. Popper took this matter seriously and began verification research. With the pair of Qinghua vases as standard, he compared them to other Chinese Qinghua porcelain in Iranian and Turkish museums. Subsequently, Qinghua porcelain with similar features as the standard pair were classified as Zhizheng Qinghua, named for their time of make. With further verification of the authenticity of the standard vessels, supported by newer archeological findings, only then did Chinese Yuan Dynasty Qinghua gain the recognition of the people.

Zhizheng Qinghua had the following general features: large sizes, stately and powerful form; brightly colored Qinghua imagery, with running ink effect; containing iron rust marks; glaze was often blue-white or egg-white color; rich subject matter in decorative imagery; and complex layout of decorative patterns, with a sense of layers. In all these unique features, the most characteristic of the gracefulness of Yuan Qinghua would be its distinctive form and the cobalt blue Qinghua imagery, the decorative motifs and subject matter.

Zhizheng Qinghua came in mostly large-sized vessels, with characteristic objects such as the Meiping vase, the slim-necked and broad bellied vase, handled-pots, goblet, large jars, large dish and so on. Its target consumer group was the Islamic countries in West Asia. Therefore, its decorative patterns and techniques as well as the shape and form of the vessels were all quite distinctive. The large dishes were usually bevel-lipped, with round or polygonal mouths. In the Qinghua collections of Turkey and Iran, as well as artifacts unearthed from India, large dishes represented a big portion of these collections. These large dishes had round or polygonal shapes. The ones with polygonal mouths were around 45 cm in diameter; the larger ones can reach 57 cm or more and very few pieces were below 40 cm in diameter. Those with round mouths had diameters usually around 40 cm; few reached 45 cm and higher. This type of large dishes is the most common type of Yuan Qinghua in existence today. However, within China, only a few museums including the Palace Museum in Beijing and the Shanghai Museum have the large dish in their collection, while most specimens of large Qinghua dishes are in West Asian countries. It was said that the large dishes were custom made for the people in these regions who sat on the floor and ate hand-served foods from the vessel. There is also a type of large-sized *bo*, or flat bowls, most often found in West Asia. It has a flare lip or straight lip design that measures 35 to 40 cm in diameters. Some smaller ones can be 25-30 cm, while the largest ones measure in at 58 cm or more. The large jar is also another type of Qinghua vessel that survived until today in plentiful quantities, and is mostly found in Japan. Furthermore, the flat kettle which has a really particular style, are found mostly in the Middle East, except for one piece at the former Yuan Capital in China. As for Meiping vases, six pieces were discovered at the Gao'an kiln in Jiangxi all at once. This discovery gave evidence that this was a type of vessel used both domestically and for export markets. The goblet was first created in the Yuan Dynasty. It was made to better serve the nomadic life of the Mongolians, thus it was rarely found in other countries and intended mostly for domestic use. As for now, very few typical household Qinghua wares have been discovered in China, such as bowls and plates and so on. The export of large quantities of Yuan Qinghua played a major role in promoting cultural exchange between China and other countries, among which, Turkey, Iran and Vietnam produced the best quality imitation ware of Jingdezhen Qinghua porcelain. Each of the countries' imitation ware possessed its respective national styling, and all are testimonies of the history when Chinese and foreign cultures came together.

Qinghua Buddhist hat-shaped pot with Tibetan inscriptions. Xuande period, Ming Dynasty. Collection of the Norbulingka Monastery in Tibet, China.

Yuan Dynasty Qinghua adopted the use of imported cobalt coloring, which consisted of low concentrations of manganese and high iron content, as well as small traces of sulfur and arsenic, and no traces of uranium and nickel. On the surface, at the parts where the Qinghua blue was concentrated, there would be black speckles that sunk into the body. These iron specks would appear on the glaze and result in an uneven surface; it was the most distinguishable feature of the Yuan Qinghua and was never to be replicated in later generations. The colors of Yuan Dynasty Qinghua included dark blue, bright blue and violet-blue, which were pure, intense and heavy, with a special kind of ink-washed effect, as if a Chinese ink and wash painting. The choices of subject matter for the decorative images were often dragon and phoenix, *Kylin*, peony, floral scrolls as well as scenes of legends and romantic takes on history; such stories included "Thrice Visiting the Thatched Cottage," "Lady Zhao Leaving the Frontier" and so on. No export Qinghua ware was absent of full bodied decorations as well as paintings and illustrations, which were all initially provided with sample drawings by the Mongol government's art offices. The painters and illustrators followed the illustrated guides and paid meticulous attention to the art works, which made many Yuan

Qinghua teapot with floral motifs on decorative window. Daoguang period, Qing Dynasty.

81

Qinghua wares in a class of their own.

In the summer of 2005, the Christie's Auction House of London held an auction. A piece of Yuan Dynasty Qinghua jar with painted figures, owned by the Dutch Van Hemert family for over 90 years, was sold for the record-breaking price of 14 million British Pounds (equivalent of 230 million Chinese Yuan), it was the most expensive Chinese porcelain ever auctioned. The beautifully painted scene on this piece of Qinghua jar seemed to come to life. The main character *Guiguzi* was depicted sitting in a dual-wheeled carriage hauled by a lion and a tiger; behind them were two horse

Qinghua dish with Sanskrit inscriptions. Kangxi period. Collection of the Museum of Tibet.

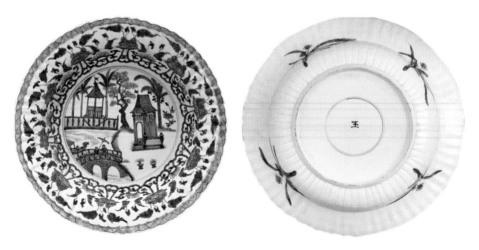

Qinghua chrysanthemum petal dish with illustration of figures and buildings. Kangxi period, Qing Dynasty. Collection of the Palace Museum.

riders, one of which wore the uniform of a military officer. The officer carried a flag with the Chinese characters *Guigu*. The story told took place during the Warring States Period in China, when the nation of Yan was at war with the nation of Qi. The Yan army had captured the disciple of Guiguzi who fought for the Qi army, thus he was accompanied by his army, going to the rescue of his beloved student.

Yuan Dynasty Qinghua was mainly intended for the overseas markets. It did not capture the interests of the literati and high officials in China. The Yuan court set up Fuliang Porcelain Office at Jingdezhen to produce porcelain solely for the court, favored the Luanbai, or egg white porcelain, made by Jingdezhen. This kind of single-color glazed porcelain continued the traditionally high aesthetic ideals of the Chinese literati, praising clean and simplicity as the most elegant beauty.

However, changes started to take place in the Ming Dynasty. The culture of the city people awakened as Chinese opera and novels appeared. This changed the aesthetic preferences of the Chinese. Qinghua porcelain, sporting white backgrounds and blue paintings, was not only a beautiful ornamentation in the homes, it can be produced with paintings of figures, landscapes, and birds and flowers; even scenes from popular operas and novels. Its ability to express and entertain was something single-colored porcelain with one layer of glaze could not accomplish. As a result, Qinghua porcelain gained recognition at home in addition to its fame overseas. The Ming rulers established a special imperial kiln at Jingdezhen to make porcelain specifically for the royal family members. The Qinghua soon became the mainstream product for all Imperial kilns.

During the Yongle (1403-1424 A.D.) and Xuande (1426-1435 A.D.) periods in early-Ming Dynasty, the bodies and glazes produced by the Imperial kilns were much more improved from before. The body was fine and white with a touch of pale blue-green; the glaze was thick and full-bodied, glistening with shine; and the Qinghua's blue color was intense. Those were the common features of porcelain in this time period. By mid-Ming, the artisans of Jingdezhen transferred Chinese ink painting created by the literati directly onto the bodies of porcelain as decoration. This act largely enriched Qinghua porcelain's forms of expression. Since Qinghua porcelain uses underglaze painting, the images were directly applied onto the unfired and water absorbent clay body. This way, the true meaning of a literati painting — the ink-wash effect was fully realized. Before this, only decorative patterns were used to enrich porcelain ware. Now that painting on porcelain was available, many wares were grazed by portraitures that were called "the transcendent ones." These were people depicted in the paintings showing their transcendental characters by either walking amidst high mountains and clouds, or feeling at ease and content. Such an attitude towards life appealed to the literati and the recluse. These paintings were usually rather impressionistic and did not focus on accuracy of shape and form. A few strokes and curves may constitute the image of a figure, with certain highlighted spots that brought out the essentials of the image. Sometimes these figures were blended in with the background, thus the man and nature became one. In addition, aside from paintings depicting lives of the literati and recluse, there were also many images of immortals and Daoists, who appeared more expressive and dominating. In the paintings' backgrounds, one can find images of traditional Chinese buildings or landscape, shrouded in heavenly aura. The main differences between portraiture found on mid-Ming Dynasty porcelain and those of the Yuan Dynasty were in both style and subject matter. Earlier Yuan Qinghua had illustrations that were very much influenced by prints which had a stringent type of brush work. Subject matter-wise, Yuan Qinghua illustrations took its themes from stories of Yuan drama or novels, with a strong sense of plot and were suitable for the common people. On the other hand, Qinghua portraitures and paintings during the mid-Ming were influenced by the literati style. Its subject matters told of the lifestyles of the literati and Daoists in a stylish and free manner, with a high sense of transcendence sought by the literati.

The quality of Qinghua porcelain, from the Ming to the Qing Dynasty, has reached a new height in the time of Emperor Kangxi (1662-1722 A.D.). The typical Qinghua porcelain used blue coloring of mostly domestic origins form Zhejiang Province. Since Qinghua adopted the new technique of calcination, it had very bright colors and the feeling of jade. In the mid Ming Dynasty, the older technique could only produce a dark and a light color. However, by the Kangxi period, in order to show smooth transitions from darks to lights, five shades in the coloring material were created. The pigments would be placed in individual bowls and used separately and never mixed. According to the needs during the painting process, the separate shades were applied to the appropriate areas of lights and darks. For this special feature, the Kangxi Qinghua was also known as Qinghua Wucai, literally "Qinghua in five colors," technically implying multiple colors.

However, by the end of Kangxi's reign during the Qing Dynasty, with developments in Wucai porcelain, and the Fencai porcelain which followed during Yongzheng's reign, Qinghua porcelain production began to thin out from Imperial kilns. However, among the masses, Qinghua porcelain was there to stay. Its speediness in production, rich decorative methods and refreshing colors gave it long-lasting favors from the people. Until this very day, Qinghua porcelain is still an important object in porcelain for daily use.

Chapter **9**

Zisha – the Taste of Tea

The Yixing area of Jiangsu Province has a long and distinguished history. Legend has it that Yixing was founded by of Fan Li, a senior official in the Kingdom of Zhao. He made a fortune making pottery there and was given the title "*Taozhugong*," or the porcelain gentleman; the kilns people of Yixing used to call him "father of pottery." However, archeological evidence shows that Yixing was already a production place of pottery ever since the Neolithic Age. The pottery of Yixing began to achieve popularity and fame after the Ming Dynasty, as one of its towns by the name of Shuye crafted the single colored, non-decorated Zisha (purple clay) pottery.

From historical records, we have evidence that a kind of "purple clay" vessel was created as early as the Northern Song Dynasty. It is easy to see the long history of Zisha, which literally means "purple sand." This type of pottery had a finely textured body, with iron contents as high as 9%. It was fired at temperatures around 1,200°C, and appeared reddish brown, maroon or dark purple. Its density and hardness were quite outstanding, thanks to the purple and red clay in the Yixing area.

Zisha ewer with loop handle, H 17.7 cm, Dia. 7.7 cm. Jiajing period, Ming Dynasty. Collection of the Nanjing Museum.

Zisha clay is a type of highly moldable and viscous clay, which can be rather easily modeled to the desired form. It can be used to make tea ware, stationery, wine ware, tobacco ware, flowerpots and other vessels of daily use, thus it is highly functional and practical. Zisha wares are not glazed, and the duo way pores in its body can be observed under a microscope at 600 times magnification. Its body has relatively high water absorbency and good diffusion abilities for air and other gases. In modern scientific studies, it was realized that Zisha pottery will let air pass through its walls but not water. Thus Zisha ware is great for sealing in the fragrance of tea, and keeping the roots of flowers and plants strong and healthy.

Squash-shaped Zisha teapod. Made by Chen Mingyuan. Qing Dynasty. Collection of the Nanjing Museum.

Early Zisha wares were usually pots and jars, with rather course bodies and rough forms. It was mainly used by the common people for the purpose of heating water or brewing tea before the name become synonymous with exquisite tea sets and elegant display ware. Roughly around the latter parts of the 17th century, Zisha pots evolved from the round or square forms to much more natural and compelling shapes which resembled

Ruou ewer. Paintings by renowned Qing Dynasty painter and seal maker Chen Hongshou (1768-1822) for ceramic production by famous ceramic artist Yang Pengnian. Collection of the Nanjing Museum.

Wanquan teapot with six facets. Daoguang period, Qing Dynasty. Collection of the Nanjing Museum.

flowers and fruits; the literati and tea aficionados loved the newer Zisha ware. These natural forms include the pumpkin pot, tree and plant pot, polygonal bamboo pot, sunflower-shaped pot, Buddha's Palm pot, river snail-shaped cup, pomegranate case, lotus leaf jar and so on. In the design of its form, both aesthetics and functionalism were considered; a beautiful design feature can be more than meets the eye. These toys of elegance came in several main categories, which were vegetables, fruits, bamboos, insects and shelled mollusks, birds and wild animals and so forth. The "melon-shaped pot" by Ming artisan Chen Hongyuan and "pot with bamboo designs and eight trigram markings" by Qing craftsman Shao Daheng are better known pieces of work today.

Before the Tang Dynasty, tea vessels and food containers weren't so clearly distinguished. As the fashion of tea drinking caught on, the craftsmanship and creativity in design of tea wares improved with each day. By the end of the Tang, the ideal tea ware appeared – the Zisha teapot. Zisha teapot was produced in Yixing, which was situated at the juncture of the Jiangsu, Zhejiang and Anhui provinces, next to the famous Taihu Lake. This was the celebrated tea production base; many prestigious types of teas were collected here as imperial tribute for the courts. The rise and development of Zisha pottery was closely tied in with tea production areas, the fashion of tea drinking, tea brewing techniques and the changes in tea ware. It is safe to say that the popularization of tea as a beverage in the Song Dynasty and the promotion of tea drinking by the literati and scholar-officials were the direct incentives in the maturing of Zisha craft.

Other well-known tea wares, such as the black glazed tea ware by Jianyang kilns in Fujian Province, also benefited from the popularization of tea during the Song

Petal-shaped Zisha pot in enamel coloring and painted gold, Dia. 6.5 cm at mouth, Dia. 8 cm at foot. Made in Yixing. Qianlong period, Qing Dynasty. Collection of the Palace Museum.

Dynasty. In the book *Chalu*, literally *The Record of Tea* (written from 1049-1056 A.D.) by Song Dynasty scholar Cai Xiang, "the tea drink is white in color, and therefore should be contained in black cups. The glazed tea cup produced by Jiangyang kilns is black in color with a hint of red and has natural, hair-thin grains in the porcelain. Its relatively thick body makes for a good way to keep the temperature of tea warm." In another area, the literati class of the Song Dynasty was often engaged in "tea battles." The Jian black porcelain tea ware became the undisputed "must have" tea ware for such activity. Therefore, the Jian kilns at one time were the special supplier of glazed black tea cups for the imperial court. One may find the names *Youdi* and *Tuhao*, two kinds of glazed black porcelain, often mentioned in ancient literary works. These were the two types of black tea ware most favored by the literati of the times. They were made in the style of the Jian black porcelain, and deeply influenced the Japanese tea arts and porcelain-making industry. The "father of Japanese ceramics," Shiro Kato, had once studied porcelain crafts in Jianyang.

Yixing Zisha tea ware started its lifespan in the Northern Song Dynasty. By the Ming Dynasty, teapot-making masters abound, who produced Yixing Zisha teapots that sported striking designs and grandness in style. The popularization of Zisha pots from the Ming Dynasty onwards was obviously contributed to tea drinking customs. Bunched tea was replaced by loose tea; water was started to be used to brew tea; and as tea brewing vessels, small cups were no longer considered clean and heat-preserving, thus were supercede by the teapot. Especially by the mid-Ming Dynasty, as people demanded more visual appeal, fragrance and taste from tea, the evaluation for teapots came to be based on the principle "small is better than large and shallow is preferred over deep." Therefore, all Zisha teapots were aimed at miniaturization with an air of elegance; the highest ideal artistically would be to have "beautiful teapot and fragrant tea." Brewing tea in small pots had been a trend since the end of the 16th century, with well over 400 years of history. Using a Zisha teapot has the advantages of slower heat loss; less chance of tea fermentation due to the ingenious air aperture in the lid so that

Guava-shaped Zisha small cup. Made by Chen Mingyuan. Qing Dynasty.

water droplets wouldn't form and fall back down into the tea; the body is highly resistant to heat and cracks, since it has already been fired under extremely high temperatures. The longer one uses a Zisha teapot, its body and shine becomes even more extraordinary; the tea brewed from it would be even more fragrant and tasty. The real knowledgeable tea and teapot lovers like to use specific teapots to brew particular types of tea, so that each teapot will retain a pure fragrance of its corresponding tea as time passes.

A unique feature of Zisha pottery, which differentiated it from other ceramic products, was its name, which was often after a famous master of ceramics; the price and value of a Zisha pottery also soared as a result. Gong Chun, a man of the Ming Dynasty was one such master teapot artist, who promoted the status of Zisha ware from an age-long traditional product to a universally acclaimed art form. It was said that Gong Chun once learned ceramic crafts from monks, and his works were the closest thing to perfection with a retrospective nature. Thus Gong Chun was suddenly known throughout the land. The Gong Chun pots became a system of pottery in itself. Since Gong Chun, mange other skillful and renowned Zisha makers emerged. In the Ming Dynasty, there were the "Three Da's (three artisans with the character "Da" in their names)," as well as Chen Yongqing, Chen Zhongmei and others; in the Qing Dynasty, there were Chen Mingyuan, Yang Pengnian and Shao Daheng; there was also contemporary artist Pei Shimin (1892-1977 A.D.). However, the originals works of these masters are rarely seen in the present day.

Since many literati and people of high taste and elegance directly participated in the design and making of Zisha teapots, thus the small wonder had, on its body, full of calligraphies of poems and prose, paintings, seal prints and sculptural elements, infusing it with high artistic and cultural values. Every piece of Zisha teapot is a collection of people's interests, emotions and attitudes towards life. What the teapot and the drink leave people with is not merely the sense of taste in the mouth; an eternal bond and love for the tea ware and tea is formed. Tea lovers all like to collect teapots. Zisha teapots from Yixing made by the hands of master artisans are worth the price of gold. Collecting teapots and refining its body and tea fragrance over time, with each use, has always been viewed as an elegant hobby.

Chapter **10**

Wucai Porcelain

Yuhuchun vase with plum patterns in underglaze red. Ming Dynasty.

The Qinghua had the artistic effects and long heritage of both bright and colorful porcelain as well as elegant single-colored porcelain. Once a Qinghua is fired and done, its colors will never fade. It is also a technique that could be adopted for both upscale products as well as the average makes. Therefore, the Qinghua stayed as the mainstream for 300 years during the Ming Dynasty. After the Ming Dynasty, however, Chinese porcelain-making shifted from producing mainly single-colored porcelain to colorful, painted porcelain, which became the mainstream product. Especially in Jingdezhen, from the foundations Qinghua porcelains, new categories of colored porcelain were developed which included Doucai, Sancai, Honglucai, Jincai and so on. The decorative graphics, subject matter and theme, techniques of illustration, craft process, tools and materials came in such a multitude of forms and fashions that were never seen before. Of the new types of porcelain, the most characteristic were the Wucai and Fencai porcelains.

Wucai porcelain was first known in the Jiajing (1522-1566 A.D.) and Wanli (1573-1619 A.D.) periods of mid to late Ming Dynasty. The name literally translated into "five colors", which really implied a multitude of colors. Wucai was the combination of overglaze colors and underglaze Qinghua. Not only were its colors bright and eye catching, its brushstrokes were also very interesting and densely arranged. It was the Kangxi period of the Qing Dynasty that Wucai porcelain reached its pinnacle of success, thus the finer pieces of Wucai were divided into two categories – the Da-Ming Wucai and Kangxi Wucai.

Da-Ming Wucai had its roots in Doucai porcelain, which was a style of porcelain that had overglaze coloring within areas defined by Qinghua outlines. The Qinghua Doucai porcelain of Jingdezhen had already been fully developed and gained a high reputation by the Chenghua period of the Ming Dynasty. By the Jiajing period, with demand from the market, Wucai porcelain began to appear. The Wucai at this time still cannot be fully distinguished from Qinghua, as there was still no true blue and black coloring. Therefore, Qinghua coloring not only had to represent blue, it also had to be doubled as black for the outline of objects. Therefore, Wucai porcelain at this time was also called

Qinghua Wucai. Qinghua Wucai relied on intricate but dense patterns that fill the entire space on the vessel. In color choices, Wucai had red, light and dark greens, yellow, purple and underglaze blue. It especially emphasizes red so that the entire composition appeared more dashing and striking, purposely seeking resplendence. The Qinghua Wucai, which became very popular, reached its maturity in production technique by the Wanli period. Due to large export volumes, Da-Ming Wucai had become a familiar product of porcelain lovers worldwide.

Da-Ming Wucai usually came in shapes and forms such as large cup, dish and plate, pot, jar, *dun*, *lu* case, *dinglu*, bowl, writing-brush washbasin, vase, zun, loop-handled pot, square ding, container box, writing-brush holder, seal container and so on. The *dun* refers to all kinds of seats; *Lu* cases were containers made of porcelain, used to store cosmetic rouge, powders, seal ink paste, pigments and so on. *dinglu*, or cauldron, was an ancient cooking container that evolved into ritualistic and display objects. The *xianglu*, or incense burner, was often used for burning incense or joss sticks. There were other miscellaneous porcelain tools, mostly toys and display items such as go pieces, screens, hat holders, writing-brush racks, writing-brush holders, inkstones, shafts of writing brushes, writing-brush washbasins and so on. In addition, there were also porcelain ritualistic utensils. Decorative patterns were mostly depictions of dragons, phoenixes, flowers and plants, as well as scenes including frolicking children, the Eight Immortals, a hundred deer and so on. From these then popular utensils, we can readily see that porcelain products have seeped to every

Tri-pod cauldron on red ground with green ganoderma patterns. Jingdezhen Imperial Family kiln. Chenghua period, Ming Dynasty. Collection of the Jingdezhen Ceramics Research Institute.

93

Qinghua urn with lid and colored fish and algae patterns. Jiajing Period, Ming Dynasty.

part of people's daily lives and were an indispensable part of life.

Da-Ming Wucai's decorative style was influenced not only by its contemporary – Qinghua porcelain, but other related arts at the time as well. The Ming Dynasty was a time of rapid development for the Chinese silk industry as many new types of silk products were being made. Silk embroidery mainly featured graphics and design patterns of plants and birds, symbolizing good fortune; as well as geometric designs. These graphic designs also grazed the surfaces of Wucai porcelain. For example, as designs often found on brocades, *tuanhua*, or designs and patterns arranged in a circular shape (local artists called it ball patterns), as well as multilayered floral scrolls on top of patterns, were decorative elements created in the mid Ming Dynasty and continued to be improved and used until the Qing Dynasty. These were the intrinsic attributes of Wucai porcelain.

In addition, Ming Dynasty engravings and prints injected fresh new inspirations into Wucai porcelain. Earliest Chinese prints from the Tang Dynasty were mostly depictions of scenes from Buddhist scriptures, as it was a period of prime influence for the Buddhist religion. The Five Dynasties Period and Song Dynasty had engravings and prints that were rather broad in subject matter. Especially in the Song Dynasty, as book publishing was a flourishing business and the advent of moveable type printing, the art of engravings and prints reached unprecedented prosperity. By the Yuan Dynasty, Chinese opera and literature, novels and story books were all highly developed trades, and were the most practically meaningful forms of art. A completely unobstructed path of development was thus paved for the art of engravings and prints. From the Wanli period of the Ming to early Qing Dynasty, the pages of all kinds of Chinese opera-turned-novels and biographies were coupled with highly informative prints. These illustrations provided a visual cue that made the plots even more tangible and understandable; they were warmly received by the readers. Chinese prints entered an era of popularity never before experienced. Many accomplished painters emerged to support the art of engravings and prints, and skillful craftsmen were there to help with the task. Engraving workshops and printers can be found in every city. Famous engraving artisans were found mainly in the cities of Huizhou, Nangjing, Hangzhou, and Beijing and so on. Of all these cities, Huizhou's engraved prints were top notch in quality and unmatched by all others. Throughout the life of the Huizhou school, some of the most talented and skillful hands were discovered. It held the highest status in achievement as a school of print-making and was a shining gem in the history of the art.

Jingdezhen is geographically near Huizhou, as business and exchange of people between the two places were intimate. The exquisite engravings and prints from Huizhou opened up a whole new realm for porcelain artisans in Jingdezhen. Since the Wanli period of the Ming Dynasty, regardless of Wucai or Qinghua porcelain, the style of its expressed imagery had changed quite noticeably. The skillful porcelain artists transferred all the qualities of prints onto their porcelain ware. The refined and highly organized lines and the clever use of pointillism to create light and shaded areas were new techniques employed in Wucai porcelain. Hence Wucai porcelain had expressive line works as well as bright and refreshing colors. Wooden engraving's influence on Wucai porcelain was more than adornment technique, it was in the subject matter as well. The wooden engravings, at the time, took its subject matters from not only popular novels, operas and biographies; there were also books of history, local records and albums of famed painters, which all gave their share of inspirations. Content wise, aside from the run of the mill portraiture and landscape illustrations, there were also images that expressed the inner voices of the literati. Scenes from popular novels that were much loved by the people were also illustrated. These story-rich and neatly presented wooden engravings made late-Ming Wucai porcelain improve in leaps and bounds. With great influences from accomplished painters such as Dong Qichang, Chen Hongshou and Liu Panyuan, many of their works were recreated in large areas on porcelain, which had well designed compositions and profound meanings.

By the time of the Kangxi period, Wucai porcelain was an even more mature and refined art form. It really had nothing matching its quality since ancient times, and we are still not able to surpass its quality today. Therefore, all the Wucai wares of the Qing Dynasty were also called Kangxi Wucai. The most prominent contribution to come out of Kangxi Wucai was the discovery of real blue and black overglaze colorings. With a real blue pigment, Qinghua blue was no longer needed as a substitute color. Wucai colors were now directly painted on the white glaze instead of on Qinghua porcelain. The intensity of the new blue coloring was far superior to those of Qinghua. The black color during the Kangxi period had the shine of black paint. When used among the images of Wucai, it strengthened the effects of the overall image. The material used for painting lines on Da-Ming Wucai was glue bound distemper, and was upgraded to

The god of longevity, Qinghua Wucai porcelain sculpture, L at base 12.2 cm, W 6.6 cm, H 24 cm. Wanli period, Ming Dynasty.

frankincense oil in Kangxi Wucai. With different properties between the old and new materials, the effects conveyed in the image were also different. Glue bound distemper is a water-based paint and not easily absorbed by the smooth and non-porous glaze. The artist must use steady and quick strokes in order to avoid leaving watermarks when the brush stays in one spot for too long. Therefore it was very difficult to create neat and controlled lines, so only a loose style of painting was suited. Frankincense oil, however, is an oil-based material which has a certain degree of viscosity and tenacity. Mixed with pearlescent pigment used for Wucai, and using a special kind of brush made in Jingdezhen, dipped it into some camphor oil, the frankincense oil would be fully dissolved and absorbed by the brush. As long as one mastered these oil properties, the brush can then be used either swiftly or slowly, painting thick or thin lines at will. This allowed for better expression of detail. With such a technique, the artisans can give their own interpretations to engravings and prints, as well as to all other types of illustrations and imagery, and apply them to the astonishing Kangxi Wucai porcelain.

In addition, the coloring employed in Kangxi Wucai was a transparent, clear as glaze, vitric pigment. This kind of pigment can let the ground color show through. But the colors lack temperateness and it was difficult to paint a smooth and even layer with this pigment. Targeting such a tendency, the artists when illustrating their images, tried to use lines instead of flat plains. In most paintings, plains are used to demonstrate lights and darks, but Kangxi Wucai relied on lines and points for gradations from light to dark. While outlines are important, the organization and arrangement of lines can be used to illustrate things such as tree trunks, leaves, flower petals, and rocks by differentiating the light and dark plains in the objects. When these lines are covered by the transparent coloring, their rich textures can still show through and make the imagery more rich and expressive and the coloring brighter and more intense. The buoyancy of the Wucai colors was also balanced by these lines. Therefore, it would be rare to find a Wucai illustration with large areas of pure color and no lines to complement. When lines were inappropriate for the subject matter, pointillism was utilized;

Wucai goblet with patterns of clouds, dragons, flowers, and birds. Wanli period, Ming Dynasty.

97

Wucai zun *with Guanyin Bodhisattva figure. H 45.4 cm, Dia. 12 cm at mouth, Dia. 14.5 cm at foot. Kangxi period, Qing Dynasty. Collection of the Jinan Municipal Museum, Shandong Province.*

such as for painting the ground or the dark sides of natural rock sculptures, using points that were either highly concentrated or gradually changing density. In Chinese, it was referred to as "sandy ground" or "plum flower dots." This technique can also be used to create exquisite motifs on the garments in illustrations of people. In short, artisans when making Wucai porcelain can rely on the crafting techniques to emphasize its strong points and avoid the shortcomings. This fully demonstrated the superiority and flexibility of the new crafting technique. Fusing contemporary painting and illustration techniques into the art, Wucai porcelain was in a class of its own.

Kangxi Wucai's material and treatment were all improved from prior products. The increased content of Kaolin made the clay paste extremely fine. The calcium oxide contents in the glaze were further reduced. New and improved kilns allowed for even higher maturing temperatures. The higher hardness and rigidity of the porcelain was never before achieved. The body felt more smooth and refined, so that the coloring over the glaze appeared even more brilliant and were a real treat for the eyes. Porcelain objects of the Kangxi period, regardless of size, were all modeled in standard shapes and intricately made.

The commoner's kilns of this period produced many large porcelain products, especially carved vessels such as *zun*, *gu*, fish tanks and so on. Their sizes exceeded their counterparts from the Jiajing and Wanli periods in the Ming Dynasty. The increased size made for powerful statements and was aesthetically pleasing. There also emerged many rectangular shaped vessels, which were not made from molds, but instead formed by mounting several pieces together. It was quite difficult to achieve, thus such kind of vessel was rarely found in previous time periods. The improvement in material and technological standard ushered in a unique artistic style. The corners of adjoining facets were obvious, and the bends were executed with certainty. Even curved lines or surfaces contained elements of straight lines or sharp angles. In such a style of harmony, the straight lines have the qualities of masculinity and strength. When used together with the brightly colored decorative motifs, it conveyed an upward and unyielding

Wucai vase with human figures. Kangxi period, Qing Dynasty.

spirit of its era – the period of Kangxi, the longest of all feudal eras ruled by a single emperor in Chinese history.

Qing Dynasty Wucai not only possessed innovations in crafting, modeling and illustrative techniques, it showed the greatest varieties in expressed subject matter of all porcelain during and before its time. The Qing rulers were promoters of Confucian teachings, advocating ruling the country with virtues and bonding the people with courtesy. This was congruent with traditional Chinese philosophy. Thus the porcelain products of this era contained much educational objectives. Stories of allegiance to the ruler often appeared in large illustrations on Wucai porcelain. These well known works included Romance of the Three Kingdoms, The Water Margin, The Legends of Yue Fei, and Lady Zhao Leaving the Frontier and so on, mostly epic-scale stories taking place in a war-torn era. Such a genre of illustrations was commonly referred to as *Duo Mu Ren*, or literally "armed general on horseback." It often had imposing manners, with the character in a splendid and exaggerated pose. This genre of Wucai porcelain was not only loved by the domestic markets, foreign countries and especially Western painters also welcomed them. Another area reflected by Wucai illustrations was the lives and hobbies of the literati and scholars.

Furthermore, there were motifs such as the pomegranate with one hundred seeds; each seed would represent a son, which is phonetically the same as the word for seed. Other images wishing well of people, such as the pomegranate, lotus, and peach, together would signify sons, good fortune and longevity. Also there were design patterns that indicated high accomplishment and prosperity of ones children, such as the mystical animal – Kylin delivering a son to the family; male children and grandchildren abundant in the family, and so on. From the Imperial kilns, the best example of porcelain imagery were the "farming and weaving" illustrations, which were meant to be an incentive to the people of the agricultural and textile industries.

By the 30th year under Kangxi's reign, the Emperor began mass-scale examinations and selections for candidates of government sits and thus promoted the Han Chinese culture. Thus poetry and poses began to appear on porcelain in mass numbers in the form of calligraphy, sometimes complemented with illustrations. The calligraphy was done in a masterful way, truly enhancing the image composition. This kind of porcelain which focused on text and calligraphy was later viewed as a unique element of recognition of Qing Dynasty porcelain.

Chapter 11

Fencai Porcelain

*Fencai Yuhuchun vase. Yongzheng
period, Qing Dynasty.*

Succeeding the Wucai porcelain of the Kangxi Period, the Fencai porcelain, which emerged at the end of the Kangxi Period, reached full maturity during the Yongzheng Period. Just as the Wucai which was also referred to as Kangxi cai, the Fencai can also be called Yongzheng cai. Being just the opposite of Wucai's strong and bright tones, Fencai was relatively soft and soothing. Therefore, Wucai was also known as "hard pigment" while Fencai was "soft pigment."

Fencai porcelain was built upon the foundation of Wucai porcelain and derived from enamel coloring. In which case lead powder was first mixed into wucai pigments and then added with

Fencai Duomu ewer with floral scroll patterns. Qianlong period, Qing Dynasty. Collection of the Palace Museum.

Guangcai flat bottle with fine crackled glaze. H 25 cm, Dia. 7.5 cm at mouth, Dia. 10 cm at base. Qianlong period, Qing Dynasty. Collection of the Guangdong Provincial Museum.

a compound of aluminum oxide, silicon and arsenic, commonly known as opaline white. The purpose of this was to intentionally tone down the hues through the translucency of the white. The ink and wash and Chinese "bone stroke" techniques, usually applied to painting on rice paper, were used to render the designs and motifs on Fencai porcelain to produce a sense of depth and mass. The hue levels were numerous and the colors were smooth and soft. Since the colors show areas of strong and light, the sense of depth was quite apparent. The body of Fencai was pure white without any impurity; some have iron contents of only 0.7%-0.8%. The images of flowers, birds, insects and fish appeared realistic and compelling. The true masters can produce quality images of "flowers that collected dew drops" and "butterflies with visible fine hairs." This fully demonstrated the meticulous detail and beauty of porcelain from the Yongzheng Period.

The advent of Fencai, where images were painted directly on the porcelain body, was very much associated with enamel coloring on porcelain, or cloisonné enamel. Fencai, since its creation, has been considered an important category in Chinese porcelain. The reason was not only for its high crafts and exquisite beauty, but more

Small cloisonné copper plate (four in a set), L 10 cm, W 10 cm, H 2 cm. Qianlong period, Qing Dynasty. Collection of the Museum of Macao.

importantly, it was the historical setting, when the new Fencai craft won both Chinese and Western support. At the beginning of the Qing Dynasty, the Manchu emperor gathered in his courts a number of erudite men from Europe. These accomplished Europeans walked the halls of the Qing courts and introduced Western science, technology and culture to members of the upper social class and intellectuals of Chinese society. These men included the French Missionary, Mailla (Chinese name was Feng Bingzheng) who was versed in the Chinese language, poetry and history; the Portuguese with proficiency in music, Thomas Perira (Chinese name was Xu Risheng); the Italian Matteo Ripa (Chinese name was Ma Guoxian), hired as imperial painter;

Italian interpreter T. Pedrini (Chinese name was De Lige) who worked in the office of translation; the French priest J. F. Gerbillon (Chinese name was Zhang Cheng) who worked as a translator, and visited the imperial palace daily to teach Emperor Kangxi the subject of Geometry; the French scholar Joachim Bouvet (Chinese name was Bai Jin), who was versed in the Manchu language and deeply trusted by Kangxi, he worked together with Gerbillon to build a chemistry lab; the Frenchman Graverean who worked in the Qing courts as enamelware artisan; F.J. Castiglione (Chinese name was Lang Shining) who entered the courts as imperial painter in the first year of Yongzheng's rule; the Chinese and Western laws expert, Italian man P. M. Grimaldi (Chinese name was Min Mingwo); French sinologist D. Parrenin (Chinese name was Ba Duoming) who accompanied Kangxi to the city of Rehe to conduct classes for the Imperial family youths; and there were many more such foreign intellectuals. They were all prominent figures in the history of Sino-Western exchange, worthy of commemoration. Each and every one of them made their own share of contribution to the spreading of Chinese cultures westwards.

At this time, all kinds of handicrafts and art works from Europe were being brought to China by ambassadors and missionaries. In the emperor's eyes, the beauty of cloisonné enamel seemed to outshine the popular Wucai and Doucai porcelains and was better suited for the lavish decorations of the imperial family. French scholar F. Fontaney (Chinese name was Hong Ruo), special envoy of King Louis XIV to China, worked in the inner chamber of the Qing imperial palace. He wrote a letter back to his country, and what followed was an entire shipment of magnificent cloisonné enamel wares at the doorsteps of the Qing courts. Since the 50th year of the Kangxi period (1711 A.D.), the Qing courts began using imported rouge red and opaline white as coloring to test-make enameled porcelain ware. Enamelware artisan Graverean was officially appointed as a member of the imperial production house, directing the research on the technique to replace enamel on copper cast with enameled porcelain. By the 59th year of the Kangxi Period (1721A.D.), application of enamel on porcelain was in essence a success; works included mostly vessels for daily

Fencai plate of good fortune; a kind of vessel for appetizers and tea snacks, also an elegant collectible. Guangxu period, Qing Dynasty.

Qianjiangcai rectangular pierced pillow ends (pair), with illustration. Guangxu period, Qing Dynasty.

Fencai Zun with the pattern of a hundred deer. Qianlong period, Qing Dynasty.

use, such as dishes, bowls, vases, pots and so on. However, the illustrations on the porcelain were not yet refined. Most of the images were the conventional ground color with floral motifs and calligraphy inscriptions. The motifs were rather simple with heavy colors that appeared a bit too solemn. The enamel used were all imported from foreign countries, including colors of red, yellow, white, pink, blue, purple, green, black and so on. Kangxi's enameled porcelains were usually executed in floral decorations. With the Western painters joining the making, the finished product was more or less influenced by Baroque style motifs and designs which were popular in Europe at the time. Such a sumptuous and lavish décor was exactly what the Qing court and palaces needed.

After Emperor Yongzheng succeeded the throne, his love for cloisonné enamel was even stronger than his father Kangxi; he even personally joined the design and illustration process of enameled porcelain. He was also keen on quality control of the raw materials, thus the enameled porcelain wares of his time were much improved from before. The bodies were spotlessly white and the enamel pigments were fine and gorgeous. Some vessels had bodies as thin as egg shells. The colored illustrations were no longer limited to floral motifs, but were more akin to the richness of traditional Chinese realistic paintings, characterized by fine brushwork and close attention to detail and meticulous colors. With added influence of the West, the painting style had an even stronger sense of layers and depth. However, the composition and layout were mostly based on traditional Chinese paintings, with poetry, calligraphy, painting and seal prints fused into one. The added delicate calligraphy and the seal prints gave the overall image a more scholarly feel. This unique fusion of styles continued its way onto Fencai porcelain, from the mid-Qing Dynasty onwards, forging a strong link between Jingdezhen porcelain decoration and contemporary paintings at the time.

Yongzheng cai was mainly a display of paintings and illustrations, complemented by engravings, prints, etchings, embossed and pierced sculptures and more. The painting style was a continuation of the elegance and stylishness of the Kangxi period, with brushwork that was even more sensitive and

Fencai dual-bodied vase with Western figures. Qianlong period, Qing Dynasty.

delicate. The composition was relaxed and uncluttered, with everything in balance. At this time, flowers and birds paintings were often influenced by Yun Shouping's "boneless" style; while landscape paintings were aimed at the wildly popular and highly recognized paintings of the Four Wang's, who were the four most praised painters at the time by the last name of Wang. Only the colors were less intense than the Kangxi period. The "armed general on horseback" genre and characters from novels were still in fashion. When images of maidservants were portrayed, it was not unusual for them to be wearing Han Chinese clothing. Their bodies and faces were slender and attractive, as slim figured females were very much in fashion at the time. In terms of motifs, floral designs were the most rich and numerous; there were peonies, peach blossoms, Chinese flowering crabapples, chrysanthemums and so on.

Imported Western coloring no longer satisfied the need for traditional Chinese painting atmosphere in imperial enameled porcelain. Therefore, the porcelain artisans of the courts began to produce their proprietary enamel coloring and eventually achieved 18 different colors and shades; 9 more than what was originally imported from the West.

Although the magnificence and unmatched sense of realism of cloisonné enamel cannot be denied, the high cost of enamel coloring prevented it from becoming popular among the masses. Therefore, it was subject to limited production within the imperial courts. The enameled porcelain of the Kangxi, Yongzheng and Qianlong periods often had markings of the year of production using blue and rouge. Kangxi enameled porcelain can often be identified with the characters meaning "Imperial Make of Kangxi" written in regular script. Yongzheng's production label mostly imitated Song Dynasty calligraphy; while Qianlong's markings added seal script characters. These

Fencai imperial ewer with poetry inscription in decorated window on yellow ground. Jiaqing period, Qing Dynasty.

were important evidences identifying enameled porcelain of the early-Qing. These types of porcelain with relatively expensive pigments and meticulous illustrations were owned by the courts only. Aside from certain pieces bestowed to officials deserving of the honor, the common people had rarely laid eyes on them. For this reason alone, counterfeit enamelware was later created; some were almost impossible to tell apart from the authentic ones.

To make Fencai more realistic and accessible for the common people, the porcelain craftsmen of Jingdezhen added solvents and snowy white into traditional Wucai, lowering the intensity of hues and the maturing temperature. Thus the brightly colored Wucai became soft and elegant. The most important pigment of Fencai was Opaline white, which was a component in a series of colors, including powder yellow, imperial pink, pine green, jade green and others, which were characterized by opaqueness, powdery effect and thickness to the touch. Opaline white's most prominent quality showed through when it came to painting detailed texture such as garments and flower petals. It was applied as a layer of under paint; when other colors were applied on top, the rendered objects seemed more three dimensional, just as cloisonné enamel images were.

Fencai porcelain had a rich selection of colors, appearing soft and delicate. Its modes of expression were more varied than Qinghua or Wucai porcelain. Through dying and shading, Fencai subject matters became more realistic and three dimensional. Therefore, as soon as it hit the stores, it received welcome from the people. It was not only the mainstream product of the Imperial kilns, the common people's kilns also produced Fencai in large quantities. Soon it superceded the market share of Wucai porcelain. The Yongzheng and Qianlong periods were the peak of Fencai development. The works of the Imperial kilns were perfect in everyway, while the commoner's kilns made Fencai that were vivid and natural.

By the time of Qianlong, since Fencai porcelain masterpieces were targeted towards the nobility and the upper class, all kinds of Fencai screens and vessels such as long-necked and round-bodied vase¡¢calabash vase and the bull-headed *zun* were very

Fencai teapot with chrysanthemum patterns on window, Qianlong Period, Qing Dynasty. Collection of the Palace Museum.

Fencai Meiping vase with floral spreads and good luck patterns. Qianlong period, Qing Dynasty. Collection of the Palace Museum.

popular. Many more innovative designs were being realized without considering the cost of development. The selections were more numerous than porcelain of any former dynasty. Fencai porcelain writing-brush pots, inkstones, writing-brush shafts, paper weights, ink paste containers, glue containers and so on, were all innovatively and meticulously crafted. The *Ruyi*, dragon head belt buckles, the snuff bottle and other traditional products made of other materials were all given their porcelain carnations. These articles were reflections of the lifestyle and amusement of the ruling class.

Fencai porcelain in the Qianlong period, though perfected in crafting and decorative technique, had forms that still left something to be desired. Some pieces were overly elaborated while others were flaunting modeling technique; still others tried to achieve both, but none were of refined taste. The feeling of lavishness was overwhelming while not enough elegance and natural beauty was shown. Some attempts at novelty even failed to retain the most fundamental qualities of porcelain. Later in the Jiaqing (1796-1820 A.D.) and Daoguang (1821-1850 A.D.) periods, Fengcai porcelain production was still ongoing and strong. However, not many quality pieces were produced. What's worthy of mentioning was Emperor Xianfeng (ruled from 1851-1861 A.D.), who personally wrote the year and make label in regular script on porcelain, was acclaimed by connoisseurs for his skilled calligraphy.

With frequent exchange of artistic styles with Europe, Jingdezhen's style of ceramics since the mid-Qing Dynasty had a complete facelift. The simplicity, elegance and robustness in the former Kangxi period were no longer; instead, a gorgeous, delicate and over elaborated style took hold as the representative court style in this last of the feudal era. Simple and natural appearance was no longer favored in ceramics, as synthetic decorations became the mainstream. This trend lasted well into the Republic of China (1912-1949 A.D.).

The formation of the Fencai porcelain style during this time had another very important factor – the arts of the common city people. During this time period, the variety of motifs of auspiciousness, commonly found on porcelain ware of Jingdezhen and commoner's kilns, all had origins of folklores and folk customs. The time of Yongzheng was when the courts sought the combined philosophy of Confucian, Buddhist and Daoist teachings, and the culture of the common city people was fast on the rise. In order to reflect upon these folk customs, the motifs of auspiciousness were able to make its way onto the orthodox forms of art within the Qing courts. Not only did Imperial Fencai porcelain sport imagery of good luck, the overall decorative style of all of Jingdezhen was immersed in auspiciousness. Popular motifs metaphorically hinted at events of good fortune such as success in career and high status; achieving financial prowess; good luck in the New Year; the continuation of family lineage and so on. These images were based on traditional ceramic motifs, popular engravings and prints, as well as other forms of handicrafts. Since the Chinese seek fullness and liveliness, the aforementioned motifs were mostly intricately detailed and brightly colored. Some porcelain vessels were even completely covered in decorative patterns and not one bit of ground color was revealed. An example would be the Fencai Wanhua Tu, literally meaning the picture of ten thousand flowers. A different approach was to avoid cluttering all the surface of the porcelain by leaving negative spaces with shapes that could resemble objects, such as a flower petal or geometric shapes.

Jingdezhen, from Yuan Dynasty Qinghua to Fencai of the late-Qing, kept perfecting its porcelain-making crafts. The application of Fencai decorations and illustrations, especially, has yielded many successful formulas. The inseparable connection between porcelain illustrations and contemporary paintings has been kept until this very day. In order to inherit these formulas of success, Jingdezhen artisans composed and passed down many mnemonic rhymes to help succeeding generations remember these formulas. One such example, tells of the proportion of the human facial features, which is divided into eight portions. The posture of the human figure is divided into head-lengths; 7 heads when a person is standing, 5 when sitting on a stool and 3 heads when the person sits cross-legged on the ground. When differentiating people by age and gender, the rule of "attractive ladies have no shoulders; strongmen and warriors have no necks; elderly men have no chests; and young children have no waists" applies. The dynamic states of people's bodies are exemplified by the fair young lady and the witty maidservant; the young gentlemen and his smart pageboy. The category of people known as *Gaoshi*, highly erudite and transcendental persons, were depicted as free and above earthly society, often found in scenes of nature and self-amusement. Aside from formulaic rhymes about people, there were also few that spoke of objects and nature, such as color schemes of the four seasons being "spring of green, summer of jade, bluish autumn and grayish winter." The ceramic artisans of Jingdezhen relied on the passing of these rhymes from master to disciple; these were words of experience and knowledge. Through diligent observations and repeated experiments, these artisans attained the most profound understanding and handling of people's gestures and expressions; even their movements and voices can be conveyed through still images. They also used backgrounds and objects to develop atmosphere, animals and props to indicate the identity and mood of people portrayed. Eventually the artisans discovered artistic laws in implementing these techniques so that the making of porcelain can be a smooth and formulaic process.

Chapter **12**

Export Ware of the Ming and Qing Dynasties

Chinese porcelain wares have been shipped to other countries as early as the Tang Dynasty; categories included Yue kilns, Xing kilns and Tang-style Tri-Colored wares and so on. By the Song Dynasty, the ceramics industry was flourishing in development, as countless products were introduced by the various kilns. Foreign demand for Chinese ceramic products increased as the days went by. The shipbuilding industry, which was closely related to the shipping business of Chinese goods, was already a highly developed discipline by the Northern Song Dynasty. Ships with 10 masts and 10 sails were built to accommodate 400-500 people and as much as 150,000 kg worth of load. The newly invented mariner's compass was put into use, as well as a full range of equipment on the ships. At the same time, The Song government set up city shipping departments in the cities of Guangzhou, Quanzhou, Ningbo and Hangzhou (the first three were sea harbors; Hangzhou was the capital and the south terminal of the Grand Canal). Personnel were dispatched overseas to negotiate trade deals, as incentives were offered for taxes over such commercial activity, even rewards were sometimes offered. By the end of the Southern Song Dynasty, the Dutch came to Quanzhou to buy, resell and ship porcelain goods; the trading prices were equivalent of gold. There were three categories of porcelain vessels exported at the time, which were the celadon, white porcelain and Qingbai. Song Dynasty porcelain crafts and technology were also introduced to other countries. There were imitation Yue and Ru kilns wares found in the Korean peninsula. Shiro Kato, the "father of Japanese porcelain," had also been to Fujian to study porcelain-making; he created black glazed porcelain ware after returning to his country.

Even though Yuan Dynasty ceramics took up only a fraction of several millennia worth of Chinese ceramics history, the large quantities of overseas orders during the Ming Dynast were an outstanding contribution. The main export wares included Longquan celadon, Jingdezhen Qinghua, Cizhou white porcelain with black patterns and so on. They not only posed influence on the ceramics industries of the Korean peninsula, Japan, Vietnam, Thailand, Iran, Turkey and others, even the painting and decorative arts of these areas were influenced by the export wares. This was an effect on Sino-foreign cultural communications that can never be overlooked.

By the Ming and Qing Dynasties, Chinese porcelain wares attained an even higher peak in overseas export. Prior to the Ming Dynasty, porcelain production took place all over the land. However, by the Ming and Qing Dynasties, Jingdezhen outshined all other areas and became the undisputed center of Chinese porcelain production. Many factors contributed to its success. The decline of many other kilns throughout China and the concentrated production of Yuan Qinghua porcelain helped to build a solid basis for the rise of Jingdezhen, where it was joined by the establishment of Imperial kilns. Natural resources were rich in the area as well, aided by ease of transport and plentiful experienced labor power. Thus Jingdezhen not only monopolized the domestic porcelain markets but also dominated the overseas export markets of porcelain. From the Jiajing to the Wanli periods of the Ming Dynasty, the production volume of Jingdezhen Imperial kilns increase many folds; commoner's kilns in the Jiajing period numbered over 900, with 100,000 potters. The ceramic goods produced, aside from being sold to Japan and Southeast Asian countries, were also sold to Europe.

The imperial ambassador (eunuch) Zheng He brought with him many exquisite Qinghua wares on his voyages west, which earned Chinese porcelain the highest of prestige overseas. By mid-Ming, or after the 15th century, as European navigation industries thrived, merchants from Portugal, Spain and Holland sailed their enormous ships, carrying full of flint stones, telescopes, horologes, aluminum wares and other goods, traded along their routes before eventually disembarking in China. From China, they purchased large quantities of porcelain, silk and tea to be resold in Europe. For these ships, the damp-resistant porcelain goods were the perfect merchandise to be shipped across the oceans. They were placed at the bottom of the ship's hold with silk and tea on top. This kind of commercial activity was extremely lucrative, and not only made the economy boom, but also induced cultural communication and friendly relations between the East and the West.

From the 17th century onwards, the porcelain trade between China and Asian and European countries progressed into a new phase. At that time, upper-class Europeans were indulged in the fad of collecting Chinese porcelain ware, which contributed to the immense increase in export volume for Jingdezhen. The Dutch introduced popular European container models and decorative motifs to China, so that the daily household porcelain made by Jingdezhen can suit European tastes even better. Therefore, porcelain decoration aside from the traditional birds, flowers, animals and people, started to include the European clan symbols, foreign writing, image of the mariner's compass, manuscripts, fountains, as well as Western landscape paintings. The models included large deep-walled

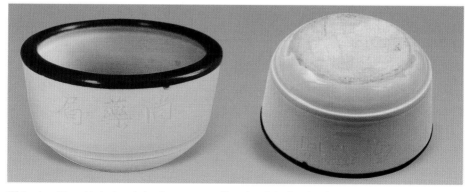

White glazed jar with the inscription "government office of medicine" under the base. Ding kiln. Northern Song Dynasty. Collection of the Ulricehamns Museum of Oriental Art, Sweden.

bowls with patterned mouths, kettles, bevel-rimmed dishes and so on. The most popular of all vases at the time was called "Jiaodeli," which was a cubic vase essentially modeled after wine flasks in Europe, with patterns of tulips on its neck. Its decorative method was very similar to other Qinghua porcelain made for the Europeans.

From 1602 to 1644, the Dutch East India Company sold over 420,000 pieces of porcelain to the islands of Indonesia. In 1613 alone, over 380,000 pieces were shipped out from Batavia to no less than a dozen destinations. The earliest surviving product order document, discovered so far, was an order placed by the Dutch East India Company in 1608 for Jingdezhen porcelain through Chinese resellers in the Malai Peninsula. The order form clearly labeled the specifications of the porcelain, including style, type of vessel, sizes and so on. These items were all specifically tailored to suit the daily living habits of the Europeans, and were shipped to Europe right after they were made. From a report on porcelain purchasing made by the Dutch inspector general in Taiwan to its Amsterdam company, we know that when he wanted to purchase porcelain ware such as large dishes, large bowls, cold beverage containers, large jars, large cups, small cups, mustard jars, wide-edged flat dish and so on, he often provided Chinese merchants with wooden models and drawings of all sorts of containers with inscriptions. These were used as references to help the Jingdezhen artisans make their porcelain to the interest of the Europeans. The export wares were also marked as specimens, which were all custom-ordered and made; paid in advance. These export-only porcelains were not used by the Chinese at all. This is also one of the reasons that many ceramic masterpieces created by the Chinese are rarely seen in China.

Amidst the porcelain trade at the time, aside from foreign merchants, Chinese merchants from Nanjing and Guangdong were all a part of this competitive arena. According to the Dutch, after the Dutch colonists seized Java, the ships of the Dutch East India Company would often come across Chinese merchant fleets docked there, who were trading beautiful porcelain and silk with the locals there. Japanese merchants were mostly deeply interested in tea, thus came to Jingdezhen to purchase ceramic tea ware. There was once a merchant in Kyoto, who specialized in Chinese handicrafts and really had a love for porcelain. He dealt large quantities of porcelain goods in his business. Through merchants in Nanjing, he requested craftsmen to make models of the best Japanese tea set from Oribe and the best water jars from Enshu, which were then sent to Jingdezhen for making of the porcelain versions.

At the end of the Ming Dynasty, with upheaval within the Ming government, the Imperial kilns ceased production. The commoner's kilns at Jingdezhen benefited from newly discovered source of Kaolin and were now free of the restraint posed by the Imperial kilns. Jingdezhen craftsmen produced products of different styles and characteristics for the particular needs of its customers. For the Japanese, since the

Oribe tea merchants and drinkers all prefer bold and unrestrained designs, Jingdezhen artisans therefore made Qinghua porcelain with highly impressionistic illustrations, as well as what the Chinese now call the Honglucai, also known as Tianqi Chihui (Tianqi was the reign title of the second to last Ming ruler, from 1621-1627 A.D.,). The rugged styles of these impressionistic Qinghua and Honglucai were highly acclaimed by the Japanese; many pieces dating from this time period are still preserved today. The Qinghua porcelain of Jingdezhen during that time had two variations – thick and thin. Those with a thick body were mostly shipped to Japan (The Honglucai exported to Japan had largely thick bodies with a few exceptions, and have created a unique bold style), while the thin bodied pieces stayed within China or were sold to other countries.

To target the European market, Jingdezhen's craftsmen created a batch of highly decorative Qinghua porcelain with exquisite designs. These porcelains came in many forms such as bowls, pots, vases, plates and more; the plates were rather numerous. Their surfaces were first divided into geometric windows of either equal or unequal areas; each area would be adorned with images of fruits, flowers and other gorgeous designs. The large geometric windows were fitted with smaller windows in between, which contained the "eight treasures," "pearl and jade" and other patterns. These geometric windows were like the petals of the lotus flower, thus were referred to by the Japanese as "lotus hands" and the Europeans called them "Clark Porcelain." At the center of the plates were paintings of still life or landscape that were rather popular then in northern Europe. There was also a type of wine flask with floral wheel decoration, which was decorated with designs of tulip on the neck, and lotus patterns on the body. Its modeling was exquisite and attractive, with a similar form and shape to European silverware. Their crafting was extremely meticulous, with thin and refined bodies. These products received love and praises from people in every European country, who were buying these items of art no matter what the cost. The Europeans, after purchasing these porcelain wares, treasured them with extreme care and love, and often fitted them with metal accessories. Some porcelain bowls were made overly thin, and to prevent burning of the hands when in use, they were fitted with a metal ring that connected the mouth and

Qingbai Meiping vase with engraved dragon and cloud motifs. Yuan Dynasty. Collection of the Ulricehamns Museum of Oriental Art, Sweden.

Xing kiln ewer with white glaze. Tang Dynasty. Collection of the Ulricehamns Museum of Oriental Art, Sweden.

117

base of the bowl; tasteful handles adorned either side. On the aforementioned wine flask, a silver sheath can be attached to its mouth and connected to the neck with a silver chain. These types of accessories not only made the use of porcelain ware more convenient, but with added beauty at the same time to enhance the overall experience.

In the first year of the Chongzhen period (1628-1644 A.D.), with a larger demand than supply of Lotus Hand porcelain wares, the Japanese tea merchants from Oribe also placed orders for something similar, which were neatly designed and illustrated, highly decorative tea ware, with certain Japanese elements. This action spurred a whole new batch of "Xiangrui" styled porcelain for daily uses. The painting technique used for these new porcelains were different from export Qinghua and Honglucai to Japan; the former being a painting-centered craft while the latter being reliant on patterns and designs. Xiangrui porcelain was more varied and unpredictable, as illustrations and graphic patterns, realistic and abstract images can all appear on it at the same time, complementing and contrasting each other. The name Xiangrui came about because these porcelain wares were all marked with the Xiangrui seal print below the base; while some had Japanese writing printed at the bottom. Some Japanese scholars believe that Xiangrui porcelain were the creation of a Japanese artisan living in China, and after being made and sold in China for about twenty years, the craft was introduced to Japan. However, some scholars say otherwise, believing that Xiangrui was the work of the Chinese and had nothing to do with the Japanese. Regardless of the differing opinions, the Chinese ceramics industry by the end of the Ming Dynasty truly inspired Japan. Many places in Japan including Arita, Imari, Kyoto and others began their own porcelain production and the wares were also exported to Europe. Especially during the early Qing period, with the newly established Qing regime still not fully rooted in the country, all international trade was stopped in China as sea shipments were banned. Seeing this as a great opportunity, Japan capitalized on the situation and created large quantities

(Left) *Qinghua military ewer with flower patterns, H 21.5 cm. Ming Dynasty. Military ewer has a variety of categories. It appeared and was exported since Song Dynasty.*
(Right) *Imitated Ming Qinghua military ewer, H 22 cm. Tokugawa period, Japan. The layout, brushwork, and pattern of its decorative design are pretty similar to its Chinese counterparts.*

of porcelain based on the Chinese products and sold them to European buyers. Even on the undersides of these Japanese made porcelain wares, inscriptions of the Chinese dynasty and years can be found. For this very reason, the Japanese porcelain craft was wide spread and prospered.

Jingdezhen by the end of the Ming Dynasty, aside from Qinghua porcelain, also produced colored porcelain, or *caici*. As explained previously, Jingdezhen produced much bold and freestyle Honglucai for the Japanese tea merchants, this was done by adding the colors of red, green and yellow on top of Qinghua, with red as the primary color. In addition, there was a new breed of colored porcelain, called the Da-Ming Wucai, literally "Five Colors of the Great Ming." Da-Ming Wucai's style was akin to that of the Qinghua porcelain made for European markets, but was also influenced by the Honglucai's free and expressive style, thus it used red, yellow, blue, green, purple and black pigments as decoration. Da-Ming Wucai was very particular and refined, enriching color composition and inducing a lavish and bold style at the same time. With already great demand domestically, Wucai of the late-Ming was also purchased by the Japanese and Europeans in very impressive quantities. This particular time period was the pinnacle of export business for Jingdezhen's porcelain from commoners' kilns.

At the beginning of the Qing Dynasty, suffering from domestic political instability, an adamant ban of the seas was in place from emperor Shunzhi (1644-1661 A.D.) on through the early years of emperor Kangxi (1662-1722 A.D.). The trade ban was lifted in 1684, the 23rd year of the Kangxi period. China also began a movement of porcelain export even greater in scale than the Ming Dynasty. At that time, China had retained the Japanese and western European markets that were status quo since the Ming; the French during Louis XIV specially incorporated a China company which purchased porcelain with French decorative motifs from the province of Guangdong. As a new customer, the Czarist Russia (1682-1752 A.D.) under Peter the Great also placed orders for Chinese porcelain. The Americas, Africa and Australia were new trade partners seeking Chinese porcelain through various channels; the Philippines, Indonesia and Malaysia were still key export markets for China. Some of these customers ordered finished export porcelain goods directly from Jingdezhen, while some ordered unfinished white bodies in Jingdezhen, to be taken to Guangzhou, Fujian, Zhejiang or other coastal regions for further process and eventually shipment overseas.

In the early 18th century, many European countries were granted the right to establish trade organizations in the city of Guangzhou. The earliest of which to receive the privilege was the British East India Company in 1715, followed by the French in 1728, the Dutch in 1729, the Danish in 1731 and the Swedish in 1732. This created for a more favorable export condition for Chinese porcelain. By this time, some countries have received the permit for direct passage and docking at Guangzhou (the permit was only temporary before), which further facilitated the direct shipment of Chinese porcelain to Europe. As Chinese porcelain trade developed, many countries established specialty stores that resold, distributed or placed orders for Chinese porcelain. According to the British publication "London Guide" in 1774, there were at least 52 of such stores in London. From the latter half of the 17th century to the 18th century, Chinese porcelain was welcomed in all parts of the world, especially in Europe, not only as daily commodities for the masses, but also as items displaying wealth. There were two main channels of outbound porcelain shipment, one through the Qing government as gifts of state to the ambassadors of other countries; the other through trade between the commoners' kilns and foreign merchants. Normally, the porcelain wares through the government channels were produced in imperial kilns, while the traded porcelain goods were mostly of commoners' production.

A considerable portion of the export wares were custom made by the commoner's kilns for the overseas markets according to specifications on the orders. Especially those products intended for the European markets, the types, modeling and decorations of which were tailored to suit the changing preferences of the Europeans each year.

With still increasing demand for porcelain from other countries and the need for more porcelain for daily use within the country, Jingdezhen's kilns regardless of Imperial or commoners' kilns met with unprecedented prosperity. They created more innovative products. Including the unmatched Qinghua porcelain, the splendid Wucai porcelain, the meticulously crafted imitation antique porcelain, and the newly created Fencai, the cloisonné enameled porcelain and so on. All of these categories were truly astounding successes.

When foreign merchants came to China, they first arrived in Macao, then traveled to Guangzhou. In the mid-Qing Dynasty, ships flocked the ports of Guangzhou and Macao, displaying a highly flourishing commercial scene. Some domestic merchants tried to cater to European tastes. They fired white porcelain in Jingdezhen and shipped them to Canton, and would then hire other artisans to imitate Western paintings and add colored painting to the white porcelain. Then by the south shore of the Zhujiang River, the porcelains were fired and turned into colored porcelain. Finally these colorful porcelain wares were sold to European merchants. An American traveler in 1769, the 34th year of Qianlong, paid a technical visit to the Canton coloring and further processing plant by the Pearl River. It was described, "In a workshop with a long span of space, about 300 artisans were painting images on porcelain wares. Different types of decorations were being affixed to the objects. There were old-aged workers, as well as child laborers of around six or seven in age. It was most surprising that there were at least 100 of this type of workshops around." This kind of processing workshop was called *Guangcai*, which made many production kilns for colored porcelain in Jingdezhen obsolete.

The large scale porcelain trade during the Ming and Qing Dynasties held not only commercial purposes; it was also a form of bilateral cultural exchange. Chinese porcelain, a form of art and culture of the Chinese, resulted in immense influence on many other countries. For example, the influence porcelain imposed on Europe was dual-phased. The first phase was from 1594 to 1720, during which Europeans purchased large quantities of porcelain from Jingdezhen. At this time, the Europeans viewed Chinese art as the most perfected art in the world; Chinese culture was the most splendid of them all; and even the political system of China was the most flawless system in existence. All in all, the Europeans looked upon China with eyes of yearning, as if it were a distant, mysterious utopia worthy of imitation.

In 1702, the Germans secretly began research and development of celadon, and they succeeded indeed. In 1710, the Germans again established white porcelain kilns. These events made Germany the first country to unveil the precious secrets to making hard porcelain. After 1720, the Europeans learned of porcelain-making techniques through missionaries in Jingdezhen, and thus began making its own mass production of porcelain. Therefore, the first phase of porcelain purchasing progressed to the second phase, a time of imitations roughly from 1720 to 1760. During this time, with admirations for China, the Europeans not only imitated the Chinese in porcelain-making, but also in architecture, furniture and glassware designs. This imitation induced the emergence of the once immensely fashionable art style of Rococo in Europe. The curator of a German Museum said in his book that Chinese porcelain influenced Rococo in very obvious ways. It was apparent in four aspects: (1) Relaxed atmosphere, freedom (a character often found in Qinghua porcelain from Jingdezhen in the late Ming Dynasty); (2) Irregular lines and curves, also similar to the freeness of Qinghua porcelain; (3) Border decorations with floral patterns and motifs (something learnt from Chinese porcelain); (4) The use of lines with high expressiveness, as this was something never before seen in Europe, but already existing in Qinghua porcelain from Jingdezhen.

The export of Chinese porcelain influenced the culture and arts of many other countries, but vice versa, their specific cultural preferences in their product orders began to direct the way Chinese design and make porcelain. Many hybrid porcelain wares with Chinese and Western elements were created. Some porcelain merchants were also artists, such as enamel artists, painters and so on. They constantly renewed their designs used to place custom orders from Jingdezhen through the East Indian Company. The

Qinghua narrow-necked vase with edged lid. Ming Dynasty. Collection of the Fundacao Medeiros e Almeida, Lisbon, Portugal.

Qinghua Octagonal Yuhuchun vase with floral patterns. Yuan Dynasty.

Swiss East India Company had its own in-house artists. One such artist was a missionary and artist specifically responsible for designing porcelain vessels which were to be made and ordered from China. Many designs of gold and silverware, glassware and ceramic products, loved by the Europeans, were directly adopted by Jingdezhen artisans in making ceramic wares. Some of these wares have been exported since the Qing Dynasty until the present from Jingdezhen, such as coffee utensils, tea wares, dining ware sets, wide-edged plates, egg-shell lamps, illustrations on porcelain and so on. Custom orders of different countries have different aesthetic standards; some required realistic renderings of flowers, figures, landscapes and architecture to adorn the surface of porcelain, while others wanted insignias of commemorative value to be applied to porcelain. All these elements gradually but surely became a part of Jingdezhen's traditional porcelain arts, quietly changing the traditional styles. Aside from the commoner's kilns, even the Imperial kilns were imitating western forms and decorative designs. These influences from foreign cultures were not only embodied in the forms, colors and decorative motifs of ceramic wares, it also created a window for the Chinese to understand the outside world.

At the time, the influenced of Western art on Jingdezhen came not only through the Western buyers, but also from the imperial court which was fond of western arts. Many early missionaries with a good relationship with the Qing Emperors were all very accomplished men in the fields of culture, arts and science and technology. They injected the most advanced European knowledge of mathematics and astronomy and the fruits of art and technology into China. On one hand, they did it out of respect and fondness for Chinese culture so as to give all-around and systematic introduction of Western society to all of China; this strengthened trust and friendly relations between them and the Chinese rulers. Emperor Kangxi, with his attention for Western technology and relentless pursuit of refinement in porcelain-making, hired French and Italian painters to take up posts the imperial kilns serving the imperial family. Their paintings styles were fully reliant upon the rules of perspectives used in Western paintings. The art of enamelware, the most classy of all handicrafts in Europe, was incorporated into porcelain-making and horology. Meanwhile, much of the porcelains from Jingdezhen imperial kilns were based on illustrations and wooden models provided by the foreign artists working for the imperial offices. These European artists even participated in the design of the Garden of Perfect Brightness (the old summer palace). The emperors Kangxi, Yongzheng (1723-1735 A.D.) and Qianlong (1736-1795 A.D.) all valued the production of porcelain wares very much. In addition to incorporating foreign artistic elements, many new forms of porcelain products and masterpieces became available. The outside culture and aesthetic standards were tightly bonded with local cultures, forging the magnificent and exquisite style of Qing Dynasty arts.

Chapter **13**

The Trade of the Artisans

1

2

3

4

5

6

7

8

9

The process of ceramics recorded by the Record of Jingdezhen Ceramics.

Pottery molds.

As for things valuable to the inheritance of the art of ceramics, aside from the surviving porcelain wares from the former dynasties, there were of course many works of writing pertaining to ceramics.

The Yuan Dynasty author Jiang Qi's book – *Taoji*, or literally *The Records of Ceramics*, though only contained a mere 1,090 Chinese characters, clearly recorded all aspects of porcelain-making and its social-economic connections, including the craft, division of responsibility, categories of porcelain, marketing and sales, taxes, exploitation by government officials, merchant usury and so on. From the book's knowledgeable contents, it is obvious that the author was not only familiar with the production of porcelain wares, he was also sympathetic to the exploited artisans. There were many references to specific time periods in the book, available for research and analysis. The *Records of Ceramics* was not just the oldest book in China on the ceramics industry of Jingdezhen, the author Jiang Qi was also hailed as the first knowledgeable man of ceramics in China by Chinese ceramics circles.

Another notable work was the *Tiangong Kaiwu*, which translates as *Heavenly Creations*, written by Song Yingxing (1587-1666 A.D.). This was an encyclopedia completed at the end of the Ming Dynasty, including subjects of agriculture and the handicraft industry. In the book, there was a chapter called "Taoshan," which mainly introduced the procedures of producing porcelain at Jingdezhen. It detailed the many steps including raw material selection, tempering, making a body, decorations, glazing, enclosing in saggar, firing in the kiln and so on. There were also limited descriptions and illustrations of potter's wheels and kilns, making this book fairly complete in scope.

The French missionary Pere D'entrecalles was the next notable figure to write about porcelain. In 1712 and 1722, Father D'entrecalles wrote two letters back to Europe, which at the time was way inferior to China in porcelain-making crafts. The letters helped to unlock the secrets of porcelain for the Europeans. With his scientific eye and basing his views on comparisons, D'entrecalles introduced the make-up, types, and ways to make early 18th century Jingdezhen porcelain. The specifics included the application and characteristics of different types of glazes; the coloring and decorative techniques of colored porcelain; controlling the maturing temperature and so on. For quantifiable material usage, capacity of kilns, as well as the length, width and thickness of crafting equipment, D'entrecalles provided rather precise numbers

The first man to comprehensively compile and detail the ceramic industry and the well-known figures in the trade was Tang Ying (1682-1756 A.D.), a Qing Dynasty man honored as a ceramic artist. Tang Ying, styled himself Jungong, with literary name Taocheng Jushi, was born in the city of Shenyang in 1682. His ancestral lineage goes back to the White Banners, one of the Eight Banners groups of Manchurians. He was 16 when he began working for the internal affairs ministry of the Qing courts.

Wherever Emperor Kangxi went, Tang Ying closely followed. He worked for the ministry of the interior for 30 years, during which he became academically and artistically accomplished. By the 6th year of the Yongzheng Period (1728 A.D.), the 8th lunar month in the autumn season, he was ordered to take office in Jiangxi Province, supervising all work relating to ceramics. When he arrived at Jingdezhen, he realized that ceramics, though being a single industry, was something he had absolutely no knowledge of. The complexity of materials, degree of fire, glaze colors and forms of vessels overwhelmed this newcomer. Therefore, Tang Ying was determined to understand the trade and quartered himself with the ceramic craftsmen for three years. During those three years, he and all others ate, worked and slept together; until he became one with the art of porcelain, fully comprehending the humanistic, emotional and technical aspects of the art. Tang Ying also indulged himself in mass volumes of literary records, searching for any and all knowledge related to porcelain-making. He organized scientific observations and studies to ancient kilns, analyzing fragments of porcelain and learning from actual case studies. Combining his findings with his readings, Tang Ying gave his all in understanding the technology, art and fruits of labor created by his forefathers.

Tang Ying was the longest serving government official in charge of ceramic crafts in Chinese history. Since he was well-learned in all aspects of ceramics including the raw clay, glaze, body, firing atmosphere and so on, the Imperial kilns in Jingdezhen serving the royal families reached a new heyday since the Song Dynasty under his guidance and design. The exquisite porcelain vessels produced were the epitome of the collective achievements in ceramics history. Tang Ying was unmatched in his wisdom to create new or rejuvenate ancient colored glazes; high and low temperature glazes alone came in 57 different kinds. In terms of forms and decorative motifs, he was able to achieve, from a single kiln, authentic appearances and bodies for retrospective imitation ware and famous wares of other regional kilns. These works contained colored images including landscapes, portraitures and figures, flowers and birds and impressionistic paintings of every possible representation.

"Tang Qinghua," a specimen for test firing of underglaze coloring of Gong County kiln. Unearthed from Yangzhou.

Each painting can be differentiated by style and its delicateness and creativity surpassed the famous works that it was based on. The porcelain wares not only achieved aesthetic and artistic standards, they also satisfied the desires of the imperial families. The quality of Tang Ying's porcelain was unmatched during and before his time. Therefore, the works made during this 28 years serving in Jingdezhen were called Tang kiln ware, universally acknowledged as the best of porcelain.

The trade of the artisan is a learning of experience. Tang Ying committed himself to the summarization and reform of the porcelain industry. He established the most complete crafting procedures in the history of Chinese ceramics, and wrote and illustrated the book *Pictorial Guide to Ceramics*; it was the most comprehensive scientific record for ancient Chinese porcelain-making. Later, Tang Ying followed up his first book with several more, leaving us all with priceless wealth.

Chapter **14**

Contemporary
Chinese Ceramics

As the momentum of industrialization caught on in China, many traditional industries changed fundamentally. From the integrated structure of the traditional handicraft industries generated many new professional areas. Today's Chinese ceramics industry is no longer monopolized by handiwork. It has been divided into several industries including industrial ceramics, architectural ceramics, daily commodity ceramics and modern ceramic arts. Regions such as Chaozhou of Guangdong Province, Zibo of Shandong Province, Liling of Hunan Province and Tangshan of Hebei Province are all newly established production zones for daily commodity porcelain; Foshan of Guangdong Province is concentrated on production of architectural ceramics. Some traditional ceramics production areas, such as Jingdezhen of Jiangxi Province, Yixing of Jiangsu Province, Longquan of Zhejiang Province, Dehua of Fujian Province, Shiwan of Guangdong Province mainly focuses on development of artistic ceramic crafts. Furthermore, those historical kilns that ceased production for one reason or another, due to market demands, have reopened for business. These include the traditional Ru, Jun, Imperial, Yaozhou, Cizhou kilns and so on. Meanwhile, under the leadership and encouragement of art institutions nationwide, modern ceramic arts have become a hot spot in the development of contemporary Chinese ceramics.

China is a nation of ceramics with a long and enduring history.

Artistic ceramic sculpture — Fossil 2004-1 (Artist: Lu Bin).

It had once directed the new trends in the world's ceramic arts. However, in the new industrial age, modern porcelain for daily use relies on Western designs and standards. Western ceramics produced solely for the sake of art, with no functional value, have only been around for a little over half a century. However, its influence on the Chinese ceramics industry is immense.

Since the 1980's, traditional Chinese handmade ceramics gained tremendous progress in development. The earliest demand for such products was from the overseas markets, as people of the world gained a long-lasting and beautiful impression of Chinese ceramic products. Even when authentic and original wares were out of reach, due to availability or cost, these ceramic ware aficionados hoped to purchase imitation ware. All at once, many traditional kilns were immersed in the production of imitation retrospective porcelain. At the same time, China's economic boom has transformed the living standards of the Chinese for the better, including furniture, home displays, interior decorations and collector's hobbies; it increased the demand for traditional Chinese porcelain ware. Although retrospective imitation is not exactly originality and creativity, it allowed for the rediscovery of many nearly lost trades and skills; and along with it many notable and talented ceramic artisans. They were immediately recognized by the market and were also granted high social status by the country.

Artistic ceramic sculpture — Owl (Artist: Zhou Guozhen)

In the field of art education, there are 54 colleges and universities with ceramics majors, with curriculums in household porcelain ware, modern ceramics, traditional ceramic crafts and so on. Many of these institutions, aside from enrolling undergraduate students in ceramics majors, also recruit masters and doctoral students. In the age-long production centers of porcelain, such as Jingdezhen of Jiangxi, Liling of Hunan, Zibo of Shandong, Dehua of Fujian, Chaozhou of Guangdong an upsurge of newly founded ceramics schools is taking place.

The multifarious cultural traditions, humanistic interactions, raw supplies and crafts of Chinese ceramic production places deeply attract ceramic artisans from around the world. The city of Jingdezhen, especially, has become a place of pilgrimage for these artisans, as it was the origin of Kaolin and the center of the

"Ray of Life" — Environmental ceramic sculpture for an art museum in Seoul, Korea. (Artist: Zhu Legeng)

world's ceramic arts. Even today, Jingdezhen's special history and culture of ceramics, as well as its unique porcelain-making techniques, are still longed for by the global ceramic elites.

The history of ceramics is the accumulation of experience and knowledge. From primitive earthenware to all kinds of colorful porcelain, the secrets of ceramics lie within handiwork formulas inherited through the generations. Even more magic is hidden in the bits of experiences gathered in various aspects of production, including material selection, producing the body modeling, decorations and firing. Contemporary Chinese ceramic arts are the most antique and traditional, but at the same time reflecting the most novel and modern. It is a reflection of the past because Chinese ceramic ware, just as traditional Chinese painting, is subject to influences and restrictions of the overall Chinese cultural history and background, in areas such as rules, laws, models, styles and inner meanings. We say that it is new and energetic because regardless of daily commodity porcelain with industrial designs or modern ceramic arts, they are all products born of the tide of industrial revolution in the Western world, and not the continuation of tradition. Contemporary Chinese ceramics bid farewell to the small and enclosed individual studios and onto the lively stage of Chinese contemporary arts. From tradition to modernity, from handicraft to expressions of individual creativity, Chinese ceramics are becoming more and more aligned with the global arts community.

Artistic ceramic sculpture —
"Savage." (Artist: Li Zhengwen)

Epilogue

Now that my writing is finished, I feel that I still yet have much more to express. However, due to limitations on the length of this book, I must stop here. The connection between ceramic arts and I is intimate and personal, because my hometown was the city of Jingdezhen. I once led a childhood life and took up my studies there. The life of the porcelain artisan was no strange thing to me as I grew up around them. After receiving my graduate degree, I taught at the Art Department of the Jingdezhen Ceramics Institute. There, I fired kilns, read about the history of ceramics and admired works of outstanding porcelain pieces by the hand of Chinese and international masters. These things were once an integral part of my life. It is safe to say that I learned Chinese history in the culture, philosophy and art domains through studying ceramics. With my learnt knowledge, when taking my Doctoral program, I further broadened my visions and expanded my area of studies. I am currently engaged in the research of arts and humanities; I find that my past research experiences helped to provide solid foundation for my work. Especially in my studies of the lives of ceramic artisans, my prior experiences proved to be crucial.

Ceramic wares were once some of the most important daily utensils of the Chinese, as "the people see food as their primal want." This was a part of traditional Chinese thinking. Confucius expanded upon the concept further by saying that "delicious foods pales in comparison to beautiful objects." This was evident that porcelain, appearing as people's dining and cooking utensil, held unmatched significance in the lives of the Chinese. More importantly, the Chinese culture has always emphasized that "objects contain the way of human conduct," which denotes that the spirit and aesthetics of the Chinese may lie within the simple objects made and used by the Chinese. For this reason, Mr. Qian Mu said in his book *A Dissertation to Chinese Cultural History* that "the arts of the Chinese are often attached to its industry; while the industries of China are often focused on the daily commodities of the average citizen. This is the point of mergence for Chinese arts and crafts and the general cultural spirit of China." "In China, industries and art forms are as one. It is reflected in the daily utensils where the wisdom and techniques of the Chinese truly shines. It makes daily life more refined and enjoyable as time goes by. This is the characteristic feature of Chinese arts and crafts." Actually, the industries mentioned here are the traditional handicrafts, of which ceramic arts are an extremely developed and typical industry. Of all the arts and crafts of China, ceramic arts are also an important form of art. From it, we not only see the types of products and its features, we are also able to witness the development and of Chinese science and technology, socio-economic development, growth and expansion of foreign trade, as well as changes in lifestyle, changes in Chinese spiritual beliefs and religion, aesthetic standards and so forth. I very much hope that my little book here had touched upon bits and pieces of these areas.

When I was commissioned to write this book, I delightedly accepted it. One the one hand, I knew of this particular craft well, I once taught Chinese ceramics history and have written the book *History of Chinese Ceramics*. On the other hand, I have a true passion for the art of Chinese ceramics, and would love to constantly savor the knowledge and information in my mind. So that I may share what I know, feel and think with all of you.

I give my gratitude to the publisher, and thank Editor Zhang Hong for her many positive suggestions and all the hard work she contributed to making this book possible.